How the Church Fails Businesspeople

(and what can be done about it)

How the Church Fails Businesspeople
(and what can be done about it)

John C. Knapp

William B. Eerdmans Publishing Company

Grand Rapids, Michigan / Cambridge, U.K.

Published 2012 by

Wm. B. Eerdmans Publishing Co.

2140 Oak Industrial Drive N.E., Grand Rapids, Michigan 49505 /
P.O. Box 163, Cambridge CB3 9PU U.K.

Printed in the United States of America

18 17 16 15 14 13 12   7 6 5 4 3 2 1

Library of Congress Cataloging-in-Publication Data

Knapp, John C.
    How the church fails businesspeople (and what can be done about it) /
    John C. Knapp.
        p.   cm.
    Includes bibliographical references and index.
    ISBN 978-0-8028-6369-0 (pbk.: alk. paper)
    1. Work — Religious aspects — Christianity.
    2. Employees — Religious life — United States.   I. Title.

BT738.5.K59   2012
261.8′5 — dc23

                                        2011027504

www.eerdmans.com

With gratitude to my friend and mentor
The Very Rev. Peter Baelz
1923–2000

Regius Professor of Moral and Pastoral Theology,
  University of Oxford
Fellow and Dean, Jesus College,
  Cambridge University
Theologian, Philosopher, Priest

Contents

Introduction

"'Forgive us our debts as we forgive our debtors.' Was I supposed to take that *literally?*" Alan was wrestling with a decision about collecting a past-due balance owed to his architectural firm by a longtime client. Facing a slowdown in business, he felt responsible for the livelihoods of his twenty employees and worried that projects were not developing fast enough to meet future payroll expenses.

A potential solution was there on his accounts-receivable ledger, an amount that could buy the firm time to generate new billings. As he dialed the number of a lawyer to pursue collection, his conscience troubled him. He recalled a conversation several months earlier in which this client had asked for more time to pay because of his own financial difficulties. Alan had been lenient then, but now his firm was short of cash, and the promised payments had not been made. "I hated the way the decision was making me feel," he said. "I wondered if God wouldn't want me to simply walk away so I could feel clean again."

Torn between obligations to his employees and to his old client, he hung up the phone and instead called his pastor to arrange a meeting. For Alan this was as much a spiritual dilemma as it was a financial and legal one, and he hoped pastoral advice would help sort things out. But when they met the minister quickly dismissed Alan's concerns, counseling him that "business is business" and to put his own interests first. Alan was dismayed. "I left his office feeling that I hadn't been heard," he said. "I don't think business is just a secular thing, and I guess I'm suspicious of anyone, pastor or not, who thinks that it is."

Alan's understanding of business is by no means unique. Many Christians believe their faith should be relevant to their daily work and are not content to leave their deepest values at the office door. Yet the world of work and even the church itself can pressure them to do just that. They wonder if it is possible to be spiritually whole in the place where they spend most of their waking hours and productive years. They are tempted to divide their lives into two spheres, one of which does not require them to take their faith seriously. For many believers, faith and work can seem worlds apart.

I believe the church has largely failed Christians who struggle daily to live out their faith commitments in their places of employment. This is a conclusion I have reached during more than twenty-five years as an educator and a consultant addressing ethics in an array of business and professional settings. Along the way, I have discovered that countless believers, like Alan the architect, find the church oddly indifferent to the challenges they face in their public lives.

Alan is a real person, one of 230 people interviewed nationwide to learn how Christians experience work and church. This research was conducted primarily by doctoral students at Columbia Theological Seminary, most of whom were working pastors seeking to enrich their ministries through advanced education. The respondents' occupations ranged from corporate CEOs and elected officials to barbers and bookkeepers. They included active members of Protestant (nine denominations) and Roman Catholic congregations in all regions of the United States. Their ages ranged from the early twenties to the late sixties; about 40 percent were female. (See Appendix A for more details.)

These eye-opening interviews are cited throughout this volume, often using the actual words of the respondents. Our study yielded two striking conclusions. First, Christians across a broad spectrum of occupations had little difficulty recalling ethical challenges encountered in their work lives. Second, an overwhelming majority reported that the church had done little or nothing to equip them for faithful living at work. They mostly perceived the church and its clergy as preoccupied with the private sphere of life — family, health, and individual relationships with God — and disinterested in the spiritual and ethical stresses of weekday work.

To be sure, not everyone has experienced the church in this way, and some emerging ministries are effectively challenging older ways of thinking about the relevance of faith to work. But such ministries are most notable as exceptions to the rule. Other people simply reject the premise that equipping Christians for the workplace is a responsibility the church should accept and take seriously. If you are among these, I invite you to read on so that we may explore this question together.

In these pages we will critically examine the cultures of business and the church, tracing some of the historical, theological, and educational influences that have led to the present situation. A tentative theological framework will be suggested for Christian life in the workplace. And we will look at the recent faith-at-work trend and consider some promising models for ministry.

I should stress at the outset that the reader will find no neat answers or prescriptive solutions here. For it is no easy thing to take Christian faith seriously in public life.

This study has led me to sources in fields as diverse as business management, church history, psychology, and moral theology. Thus I acknowledge that I cannot claim expertise in every subject area that must be considered here. I can only hope that my use of these sources is appropriate to the work at hand.

What Is at Stake?

A large body of research tells us that the vast majority of Americans want their work to amount to more than a paycheck. From a young age, most of us are encouraged to imagine our future selves in fitting and fulfilling careers. We may dream of being firefighters, farmers, or physicians. Yet even if we do not land the job of our youthful dreams, we may nonetheless find that work rewards us with friendships, personal pride, and a sense of purpose. Our weekday occupations are the primary venues where most of us serve others and develop our God-given abilities.

Of course, it doesn't always feel this way. Work can drain energy and strain patience. Coworkers can be difficult. Job security may be undermined by forces beyond our control. Unscrupulous people often excel, even as integrity, humility, and hard work go unrewarded. In a culture where identity and self-esteem are so closely tied to our careers, we strive for authenticity amid pressures to conform. There are many days when the Christian life is more easily lived at home than at work.

As believers strive for coherence across all areas of their lives, much is at stake for the church. Membership and attendance are eroding in the United States and other Western countries, even as congregations stubbornly invest their hopes and resources in traditional Sunday programs. Church priorities continue to tilt heavily toward private faith and away from ministries that might equip believers for a robust public faith. Crucial questions about vocation and money — central in so many lives today — are met with indifference, confusion, or even hostility.

In failing to bridge faith and work, the church has failed itself and society with far-reaching consequences, for the challenges facing business, government, and other sectors in the twenty-first century raise profound questions about the purposes of our institutions, the value of human beings, and the criteria for good work. These are *ethical* questions having to do with how we ought to live, collectively and individually. Yet the moral terrain of our work lives is mostly defined by law and economics rather than theology, leaving us with an uninspired ethical pragmatism lacking in wisdom and heart. How would things be different if believers at work learned to tap the wellspring of Christian wisdom? What if these Christians were to "make themselves instruments of grace," as Pope Benedict XVI envisioned in his 2009 commentary on the economy?

The issues addressed by this book are not new, but they have never been more pressing. It is time for the church to come to grips with its neglected responsibilities. It is time to close the dangerous chasm separating the worlds of faith and work.

JOHN C. KNAPP
Birmingham, Alabama

PART I

WORLDS APART

CHAPTER ONE

The World of Business

Here is a little thought experiment. What comes to mind first when you hear the word *business?* This morning's financial headlines? Your bank balance? If your daily work is in business, you may think of experiences and relationships that define much of your life.

Now consider another word: *faith.* What images emerge? It is likely your mind turned in another direction, toward God, prayer, family, and church.

This simple exercise says much about the issues explored in this book. During the seminars I have conducted in churches since 1992, I have found it useful to divide people into two groups: one generates a top-of-mind list of words and phrases associated with business, while another, meeting separately, jots down concepts associated with faith. Neither group knows what the other is doing, but the lesson becomes clear when everyone reconvenes to post their work on large sheets of paper at the front of the room. Seldom does even one word or phrase appear on both groups' lists, though the items may number several dozen. Indeed, many of the concepts deemed *most* central to faith (e.g., God, love, prayer, forgiveness) are never associated with business, underscoring just how far apart these worlds seem to be. (See Figure 1.1 for typical examples.)

Is this just a matter of semantics, or is something more at stake? What do these word associations say about the values and

---

Figure 1.1. Different Worlds?

Business	Faith
Money	God
Workplace, Customers	Church, Family
Meetings, Memos	Prayer, Reflection
Ambition	Humility
Sources of Stress	Refuge from Stress
Competition	Love of Neighbor

---

assumed purposes of each context? In the parlance of business, words like *love* and *humility* may seem of little value when speaking of maximizing profits or beating the competition.

In his book *A Better Way to Think about Business,* the late business philosopher Robert Solomon, a student of business jargon, speaks of having been struck by the imagery that peppers many presentations and advertisements. "Again and again we hear business described as a jungle, a fight for survival, a dog-eat-dog world, a game defined by its so-called winners and losers."[1] This is how many of my business students see it, but Solomon rightly contends that if such language actually reflected the way most people experience business, society would have every reason to question its legitimacy.

Fortunately, business life is not always so hard-edged, even if it is often portrayed this way. As Solomon points out, "We hear too little about the virtues of business life, about the ways in which business and personal integrity support and reinforce one another, perhaps because it makes for such boring and uneventful stories — just modest success and good feelings, camaraderie, mutual pride, and enjoyment."[2]

---

1. Robert C. Solomon, *A Better Way to Think about Business: How Personal Integrity Leads to Corporate Success* (Oxford: Oxford University Press, 1999), pp. 4-5.

2. Solomon, *A Better Way to Think about Business,* p. 5.

Yet language does matter, for it not only describes reality — it shapes it. Several years ago, I was with the management team of a large public company as they discussed cost-cutting measures in the face of mounting losses. For several hours, the firm's financial executives presented their plans in a detached and clinical manner, showing that closing a number of operating locations would reduce "head count" and yield much-needed savings. As they finished, Bob, the company's chairman and CEO, drew his chair closer to the conference table, leaned forward, and said firmly, "I know we have no choice but to proceed with these layoffs. But in deciding how to go about it, let's remember that we love these people." An awkward silence fell over the room, as if an unexpected guest had intruded on a family discussion. *Love?* I could not recall ever hearing the word in a corporate meeting, and I suspected I was not alone.

I thought about Bob's words for weeks afterwards. They reminded me of the mantra of management sage Peter Drucker: "Management is about human beings." In effect, Bob had taken a straightforward plan for cutting costs and complicated it immensely by insisting that people losing their jobs should be treated with love. Still, the tone of the meeting was entirely different from that moment on. The conversation turned from calculations of head count to creative ways to ease difficult transitions for real people with real families and financial needs. Later, when I asked Bob about this, he shrugged it off as unremarkable. "I'm a Christian," he said. "That's no secret around here. I remind our managers that faith, hope, and love should define the way we do business. But at a time like this, that's easier said than done."

"Park it at the door"

Many believers have discovered that taking faith seriously at work can indeed make life more difficult. This is due in part to a business culture that often discourages religious expression in the workplace. Executive search consultants and university career offices advise job seekers to purge their resumes of any mention of faith interests, even church-related humanitarian projects. Employer policies restrict or prohibit religious symbols and activities. The prevailing culture suggests that faith is a private matter that should not be taken too seriously in public life. "The consistent message of modern American society is that whenever the demands of one's religion conflict with what one has to do to get ahead," says Yale law professor Stephen Carter, "one is expected to ignore the religious demands and act . . . well . . . *rationally*."[3]

A national study of spirituality in corporate America by Ian Mitroff and Elizabeth Denton found that most companies believe in "walling it off as strictly as they can."

> The usual way in which organizations respond to spiritual matters and concerns of the soul is by declaring them inappropriate or out of bounds. Conventional wisdom holds that spiritual matters and concerns are far too personal and private to be broached directly in the workplace, the most public and communal of settings. Moreover, because people differ sharply in their responses to such concerns, merely raising them will lead only to acrimony and division and not to the ultimate end of bringing people closer together at work.[4]

More often than not, park-it-at-the-door thinking has less to do with hostility to faith than with the avoidance of risk, for many employers fear that any hint of religion is a potential source of conflict or litigation. To be sure, inappropriate religious conduct can lead to claims of discrimination and harassment, and in recent years employee lawsuits on these grounds have outpaced all other complaints against employers under Title VII of the 1964 Civil Rights Act in the United States. But nota-

3. Stephen L. Carter, *The Culture of Disbelief: How American Law and Politics Trivialize Religious Devotion* (New York: HarperCollins Publishers, 1993), p. 13.

4. Ian I. Mitroff and Elizabeth A. Denton, *A Spiritual Audit of Corporate America: A Hard Look at Spirituality, Religion, and Values in the Workplace* (San Francisco: Jossey-Bass, 1999), p. 5.

ble within this trend are growing numbers of cases alleging failures by employers to *allow* the exercise of faith at work. Religious freedom enjoys a special place in American jurisprudence, and the law places an affirmative burden on employers to "reasonably" accommodate religious expression and practice. Thus, employers now face the conundrum of how to prevent discrimination and harassment while leaving room for the reasonable exercise of religion as more employees of all faiths insist on bringing their beliefs to the office or the shop floor.

Over the last decade, many large employers have established formal diversity programs, complete with dedicated staffs and budgets, to deal proactively with differences in race, ethnicity, gender, and other workplace demographics, usually in hopes of promoting inclusion and removing barriers to participation and advancement. Yet few of these programs address religious issues effectively. I led a workshop for The Conference Board, a global association of businesses, where chief diversity officers of major corporations admitted they had yet to address religious diversity with coherent policies or training. "Religion is the final frontier," said an executive with a Fortune 50 company, explaining that its place in the workplace is uncertain and poorly understood. These executives agreed that leaders of their firms were more likely to see religion as a threat to workplace harmony than as an essential and inseparable dimension of many employees' lives, even though studies say the vast majority of business leaders in the United States adhere to some religious faith.

In Chapter Seven we will return to this subject as we consider the efforts of some employers to provide opportunities for religious expression; however, it is not the purpose of this volume to delve too deeply into issues of law or corporate policy. Our point here is that the cultures of many workplaces effectively relegate faith to the private, off-hours sphere, contributing to the individual's inner difficulty in holding these two worlds together.

Our Changing Relationship with Work

With a scope of influence that arguably exceeds that of the church, business is the primary locus of human interaction and relationships for millions of people. Whether you are in business, government, social services, or any other sector, the last decade has almost certainly brought some dramatic changes in how you do your own work. Change is only accelerating, mobility is increasing, and the future of your career is likely less predictable than you once thought. Relentless communication demands the constant attention of professionals and truck drivers alike, as cell phones, e-mail devices, and the Internet make it possible to stay connected to work 24/7. Meanwhile, the boundaries that traditionally separated office and home are blurred by telecommuting arrangements and by online social networks where relationships from work, church, family, and neighborhood often overlap. Your computer and mobile phone may be points of convergence for an incredibly wide range of concurrent relationships and interests. The line is further blurred by a "Millennial Generation" (born in the 1980s and 1990s) that is less willing to be defined by institutional affiliations.

We must not underestimate the significance of these changes, for they are unsettling the social structures that have divided public life and private life in Western society for two centuries. Even as workplace cultures eschew religion, Christians are finding it harder to treat their employment as a neatly bounded compartment where the claims of faith should not apply. In some ways our relationship to work is becoming more like that of earlier times, before the social transformation of the Industrial Age began to fracture personal wholeness by driving a wedge between home life and work life.

Today's difficulty reconciling faith and work must be understood as a product of long-term trends that have diminished the portion of our selves that goes to work. Beginning in the late eighteenth century, the Industrial Revolution not only changed national economies; it profoundly affected how millions of people made their livings. For prior generations, work on the farm or in the shop was close to home and often involved family members. Many people spent years learning crafts or trades and had meaningful connections to the things they produced. As steam-powered factories with capacities for mass production began to displace cottage industries, countless workers were drawn to industrial and assembly-line jobs in urban areas. This movement separated work from home as never before; long hours at the farm, bakery, or blacksmith shop were traded for twelve-hour shifts in factories or mills; the natural rhythms of sowing and harvesting were replaced by rigid daily schedules set by others. The personal connection to end products was mostly lost, for broad know-how was unnecessary for the narrower, repetitive tasks of modern systems based on divisions of labor.

For many, work became less human — and less humane — as employers came to view workers, often including children, as replaceable cogs in their great machines. To ensure maximum efficiency and productivity, a managerial class emerged to populate industrial bureaucracies, the complexity of which had previously existed only in governmental and military organizations.

By the late nineteenth and early twentieth centuries, the searing critiques of Karl Marx and others gave rise to the labor movement and the gradual adoption of social reforms in Europe and America. Yet even as these changes corrected some of the abuses of early industrialization, new transportation developments — first railroads, then automobiles and airplanes — further distanced work from home. Widespread electrification and the introduction of time-saving appliances made it possible for more people, especially women, to spend less time at home. Over the course of the twentieth century, farm employment in the United States declined from nearly 40 percent to less than 3 percent, while service industries replaced the industrial sector as the generator of most new jobs. As the Information Age dawned, Western nations were eagerly assuming post-industrial roles in a stratified global economy.[5]

5. Donald M. Fisk, "American Labor in the 20th Century," *Compensation and Working Conditions* (Fall 2001).

Meanwhile, twentieth-century educational institutions encouraged the professionalization of management and the development of ever more efficient production and distribution methods. Business courses extolled the benefits of Taylorism (originated by industrial engineer Frederick Winslow Taylor), which separated work execution and work planning, fragmented jobs to minimize skill requirements and learning time, and introduced "scientific" control of time and motion.[6] From the executive suite to the assembly line, corporations required greater specialized knowledge and technical skills.

Similar effects were felt in governmental agencies, smaller businesses, hospitals, professional firms, and other organizations. Although these developments were accompanied by improvements in pay, benefits, and equal opportunity, they inevitably circumscribed individuals' roles in the workplace. Whether a purchasing manager, a machine operator, a cashier, or a telemarketer, today's employee is less likely to have a personal connection to the end products or final results of his or her efforts, further alienating much work from a larger sense of purpose.

The Ethical Dimension

For believers this alienation is felt most acutely when workplace situations involve conflicting values. It is easy to imagine Bob's angst when faced with a choice between the expectations of his shareholders and the well-being of his employees — a hard decision made more difficult by taking seriously the Christian imperative to love others. Robert Jackall, a sociologist who has studied corporate cultures, finds that while religious affiliation is often viewed as a sign of respectability in business, the "principal moral gauges for action" are invariably defined by employers' internal rules and culture. Thus it may be out-of-bounds to speak

6. Frederick Winslow Taylor, *Principles of Scientific Management* (New York: Harper & Bros., 1911).

of the requirements of faith even if everyone present adheres to the same beliefs in their private lives. On most days, this separation may seem to be a pragmatic compromise with the realities of modern business, but it is more difficult to accept in ethically challenging moments when believers sense that the teachings of their faith should offer guidance.

Especially troubling at such times is the absence of support from the church. Our national study of Christians in non-church occupations (see the list in Appendix A) revealed deep disappointment in the church for failing to help them relate their faith to their work. "I feel like my church has a norm that business doesn't belong in church," said a retail manager. "There is the occasional joy of a promotion, or a shared concern about unemployment, but never teaching or conversation about one's faith in the workplace." Others made similar comments to the effect that the faith-work connection is seldom a serious topic of discussion or study at church. A financial planner summed up the experience of many: "The church teaches me to live as a Christian, but I have to apply those principles to my life and work on my own."

Our respondents had little trouble recalling ethical difficulties they had encountered in relationships with coworkers, employers, subordinates, customers, suppliers, business partners, and others. They described a breathtaking variety of issues — more than seventy different types of problems including financial fraud, product safety, racial discrimination, conflicts of interest, employee dismissals, bankruptcy, tax evasion, privacy violations, fair pricing, debt collection, resume fraud, and sexual harassment, among others. (See a list of issues in Appendix B.) Here are a few examples:

A sales representative for a television station felt conflicted about selling advertising to sponsor programming with content he considered sexually exploitive.

A hospital employee worried that elderly, low-income patients were often neglected and given less post-operative care than others, an inequity accepted by her coworkers as "just the way the system works."

A store manager was ordered by the corporate headquarters to reduce the number of full-time workers at her location, making it her responsibility to decide which employees would lose their jobs.

The owner of a failing business struggled to meet his obligations to creditors, employees, and suppliers, while privately weighing the option of a bankruptcy filing.

An employee of a small business discovered that his boss, the owner, was increasing the amount of an insurance claim for water damage by adding undamaged, obsolete inventory to the list of goods that were legitimately damaged.

An investment adviser faced daily temptations to boost his commission income by recommending unnecessary transactions to his clients.

For most people we interviewed, these situations and others like them were accompanied by significant personal stress. Many also found them *spiritually* vexing, as they sought to apply Christian values and teachings in practical ways. "Looking back, I made the wrong decision," one confessed, "which makes me wonder, How strong is my faith?" A health-care manager who was pressured to cut corners in order to achieve goals said, "I reached my breaking point when I could no longer sell my soul for economic reasons."

Despite a widely shared belief that faith should inform ethical decisions at work, a mere 18 of 230 respondents had ever consulted a pastor for advice about a work-related matter. Of these, six were dissatisfied with the experience, including an entrepreneur who angrily moved his church membership when a pastor made light of his concern that his product might be bad for children; nine others had sought advice only when looking for a job. More revealing were the views of more than 200 people who had never looked to a pastor for counsel in a business or career matter, a reluctance we will examine in the next chapter.

Perhaps it would be easier for believers if they could find ways to avoid this stress altogether. In a famous *Harvard Business Review* article, published in 1969, Albert Carr proposes that we simply get comfortable with the idea that the worlds of faith and work are best kept apart. He advises businesspeople to see themselves as "game players" whose actions in the workplace cannot be expected to agree with the morality of their personal lives. "The ethics of business are game ethics, different from the ethics of religion," he argues. "That most businessmen are not indifferent to ethics in their private lives, everyone will agree. My point is that in their office lives they cease to be private citizens; they become game players who must be guided by a somewhat different set of ethical standards."[7]

Carr uses the word *bluffing* to refer to "conscious misstatements, concealment of pertinent facts, or exaggeration" — all of which, he believes, are "opportunities" permitted under the rules of the business game. He acknowledges, however, that some businesspeople cannot become effective game players as long as they worry about actions that violate their moral or faith commitments. "But here and there a businessman is unable to reconcile himself to the bluff in which he plays a part. His conscience, perhaps spurred by religious idealism, troubles him. He feels guilty; he may develop an ulcer or a nervous tic."[8]

Carr's remedy? Accept that business is like a poker game, for "no one expects poker to be played on the ethical principles preached in churches." In poker, the object of the game is to go home with as much of the other players' money as possible, using whatever guile or deception may be needed to win. It is "up to the other fellow to protect himself":

> Poker's own brand of ethics is different from the ethical ideals of civilized human relationships. The game calls for distrust of the other fellow. It ignores the claim of friendship. Cunning deception and concealment of one's strength and intentions, not kindness and openheartedness, are vital in poker. No one thinks any worse of poker on that account. And no one should

7. Albert Z. Carr, "Is Business Bluffing Ethical?" *Harvard Business Review,* January-February 1968, pp. 144-45.

8. Carr, "Is Business Bluffing Ethical?" p. 145.

think any worse of business because its standards of right and wrong differ from the prevailing traditions of morality in our society.[9]

When I have business students read this article, many heartily agree with Carr's arguments. Invariably I must go to some lengths to show that business is not a game, that real-life cards are not always shuffled and dealt fairly, and that the actions of a few business "players" can affect the lives of many people who don't even have a place at the table.

While Carr would have Christians learn to move comfortably between two separate spheres of personal identity, many theologians consider such maneuvers dangerous. Theologian Helmut Thielicke, for one, condemns any attempt to limit God's interests to the private, inward life or withdraw the "lordship of God from the 'worldly' sphere."[10] Acknowledging God's sovereignty over all areas of life leaves little room for the comfortable compromise Carr suggests.

The Necessity of a Christian Ethic

Just as individuals struggle with ethical challenges at work, ethics has also come to the fore as a high-priority interest of businesses, governments, non-profits, and professions. Unprecedented attention has been given to the development of conduct codes, values statements, training programs, ethics hotlines, and other methods of establishing and enforcing standards of employee and institutional conduct. Most major corporations had no ethics codes as recently as 1990; nearly all have them today. The impetus for these initiatives comes mostly from legislative and legal reforms like those prompted by corporate financial scandals involving major U.S. companies (e.g., Enron, WorldCom, HealthSouth, Tyco, and so on).

9. Carr, "Is Business Bluffing Ethical?" pp. 145, 144.

10. Helmut Thielicke, *Theological Ethics*, vol. 1, ed. William H. Lazareth (Philadelphia: Fortress Press, 1966), p. 8.

Publicly held companies, and many private ones, have taken steps to align their practices with the requirements of the Sarbanes-Oxley Act, the recently revised Federal Sentencing Guidelines for Organizations, and the tighter rules of the stock exchanges — measures that aim to prevent misconduct, eliminate conflicts of interest, and make leaders more accountable. A new profession of ethics and compliance officers has emerged to manage conduct in large organizations; leading consulting firms offer services in ethics management; and universities are rolling out a bevy of new courses in professional ethics and corporate responsibility.

On the whole, all of this is encouraging and is resulting in some positive changes in the business community and beyond. In my own work of helping businesses and other organizations, I have met few people who doubt the need for such efforts. Virtually everyone accepts that ethical conduct should be a high priority, though many confess that workplace discussions of ethics tend to be off-putting or threatening. Today's corporate ethics programs generally articulate some positive values — honesty and fairness, for instance — but in the end, employees understand that the primary aim is to prevent wrongdoing and help the firm get through the day without a lawsuit or an indictment. Internet giant Google sums up its ethical policies in three words: "Don't be evil."

The ethical pragmatism of the business world asks not what is pleasing to God, but what will make financial gain possible. Complying with laws, regulations, and contracts is essential for any employer, and larger enterprises must work especially hard at this. But the typical corporate ethics program will not infuse work with deeper meaning, or provide wisdom for human relationships, or help employees apply faith teachings to practical decisions.

"Part of the problem is that our society isn't comfortable with faith in the workplace," said one of our interviewees, a fundraising consultant. "Very often ethical issues are governed not so much by individual faith as by governmental regulation or professional codes of ethics."

This point was reinforced several years ago when Ed Zinbarg, a retired top executive with the Prudential Life Insurance Company, spoke to an audience of business leaders about the relevance of religious teachings in today's business world. "I urge you to consider that there has been an important missing element in most books, seminars, and other discussions of business ethics," he told them. They lack "the wisdom of thousands of years of religious insight" about work and commerce. He expounded on a variety of principles and lessons from the Old and New Testaments.[11] (Zinbarg, who is Jewish, devoted his retirement to studying the business-related teachings of major religious traditions.) The audience was appreciative of his presentation, but their questions revealed an underlying discomfort. "I don't disagree with you in principle," one executive began, "but do you really think it is advisable for a global company like ours to talk about religion in an employee ethics seminar? That's best left to each individual."

If most employers see faith as a private matter — even in the realm of ethics, where it might motivate good conduct — shouldn't individuals be content to accept this? Why not take Carr's advice — learn to park faith at the door and pick it up again at quitting time? The simple answer is that such moral relativism is untenable for Christians who seek wholeness in all areas of life. The world of work is where the Christian life must be lived if it is to be lived at all.

Princeton researcher Robert Wuthnow finds that individuals' faith actually "plays a more important role in guiding work than has generally been acknowledged," but he sees that this influence is diminishing as Christianity becomes less a guide for living than a "way of making us feel better about ourselves."[12] A theologically informed ethic is necessary so that beliefs about God may ground convictions about what is right, what is good, what is true. We turn to our theology, not law or economics, with the big questions about who we are and how we ought to relate to others and the world we inhabit.

11. Edward Zinbarg, "What Can the World's Religions Tell Us about Ethics in Business?" in *Leaders on Ethics: Real-World Perspectives on Today's Business Challenges*, ed. John C. Knapp (Westport, Conn.: Praeger Publishers, 2007), p. 40.

12. Robert Wuthnow, *God and Mammon in America* (New York: The Free Press, 1994), p. 39.

The Influence of Business Education

Our discussion of the world of business would be incomplete without considering how formal education shapes the values and cultures of today's workplaces, not just in business but across most employment sectors. The professionalization of management in the latter half of the twentieth century owes much to a proliferation of university business courses and degrees, most notably the Master of Business Administration (MBA), which by the 1980s had become a virtually indispensable credential for many who aspire to executive leadership roles. MBA graduates wield considerable influence in large organizations, establishing and legitimizing management procedures, modes of thinking, and patterns of behavior to which all employees must adhere. The teachings of MBA programs thus affect far more people than actually take collegiate business courses or work in for-profit enterprises.

This influence came under sharp criticism in 2008 and 2009 as the toll of deceptive investment schemes and irresponsible lending practices precipitated a global financial crisis. A column in *The Wall Street Journal* — with the headline "How Business Schools Have Failed Business" — called for "rethinking" business education.[13] *The Guardian* in London observed, "It is business schools, after all, which flooded the banking world with graduates of their prestigious MBA courses. They then helped the economy to nosedive."[14] An online forum of *BusinessWeek* magazine featured two Harvard Business School professors who conceded that "business schools need to accept some responsibility,"[15] while some other

13. Michael Jacobs, "How Business Schools Have Failed Business," *The Wall Street Journal*, 24 April 2009; accessed online at http://online.wsj.com/article/SB124052874488350333.html.

14. Adam James, "Academies of the Apocalypse," *The Guardian*, 7 April 2009, accessed online at http://www.guardian.co.uk/education/2009/apr/07/mba-business-schools-credit-crunch.

15. Jay Lorsch and Rakesh Khurana, "Financial Crisis: Blame B-Schools," *BusinessWeek*, 24 November 2008, accessed online at http://www.businessweek.com/debateroom/archives/2008/11/us_financial_cr.html.

business scholars began to push for substantive changes in curricular content and priorities.

Similar allegations of culpability arose in 2002 as financial scandals came to light at major corporations whose names are now infamous. At that time I chaired a group called the Southeast Consortium on Business Ethics Education, comprising business deans, university presidents, and other leaders from a dozen institutions. Recognizing that some of the worst crimes making business headlines were perpetrated by executives with degrees from America's finest universities, we brainstormed ways to strengthen the ethics content of our curricula and even invited several corporate CEOs to meet with us. Like many of our counterparts around the world, we agreed that business schools must place significantly greater emphasis on personal and corporate responsibility across the curriculum. We also recognized that change would not come easily.

Yet even progress toward more intentional and comprehensive ethics education may not suffice to calibrate the moral compasses of future managers. "Business schools do not need to do a great deal more to help prevent future Enrons," argues Sumantra Ghoshal, an eminent scholar at London Business School until his death in 2004. "They need only to stop doing a lot they currently do. They do not need to create new courses; they need to simply stop teaching some old ones."[16] He rightly shows that "by propagating ideologically inspired amoral theories, business schools have actively freed their students from any sense of moral responsibility."[17] This artificial separation of ethics and economics was unknown until recent times, as economist and Nobel laureate Amartya Sen explains:

> The early authors on economic matters, from Aristotle and Kautilya (in ancient Greece and ancient India respectively —

16. Sumantra Ghoshal, "Bad Management Theories Are Destroying Good Management Practices," *Academy of Management Learning and Education* 4, no. 1 (2005): 75.

17. Goshal, "Bad Management Theories Are Destroying Good Management Practices," p. 76.

the two were contemporaries, as it happens), to medieval prac-
titioners (including Aquinas, Ockham, Maimonides, and others), to the economists of the early modern age (William Petty,
Gregory King, François Quesnay, and others) were all much
concerned, in varying degrees, with ethical analysis. In one way
or another, they saw economics as a branch of "practical reason," in which concepts of the good, the right, and the obliga-
tory were quite central.[18]

It was only in the late twentieth century that management
theories — springing from the *Homo Economicus* assumptions
of neoliberal economists like Milton Friedman (also a Nobel laureate) — began promoting an oddly constricted conception of
human nature and purpose. By regarding people solely as self-
interest maximizers who can be predicted to make decisions
strictly on the basis of rational economic criteria, business education infused corporate culture with a philosophy that left little
room for altruism, love of neighbor, or the subordination of self-
interest for the sake of others.

It is hardly surprising, then, when managers fail to consider
how their actions may impact people who are powerless to affect
their immediate financial interests. A culture steeped in the economic theories espoused by many of today's business educators
inevitably sees other-regarding actions, especially those that
may come at a cost to oneself, as alien and less than rational.
The poker game, after all, must be about pursuing one's own interest at the expense of others.

As an aside, the origin of contemporary theories lauding self-
interested behavior is usually traced to Adam Smith, the "father of
modern economics," whose 1776 treatise *The Wealth of Nations*
shows how free markets may best serve the interests of society.
What is frequently overlooked, however, is that Smith was a philosopher who believed individuals and communities must rely on
"moral sentiments" to keep self-interest in check. Smith thought

18. Amartya Sen, "Does Business Ethics Make Economic Sense?" *Business
Ethics Quarterly* 3, no. 1 (1993): 45.

that the inner pain of violating one's moral obligations should out-weigh the pleasure of capriciously indulging one's passions or greed. Whether or not this is a fair assessment of human nature, it is certain that Smith would not abide classroom teaching that pro-motes amoral, solely self-interested approaches to management.

In recent decades, the partition dividing business and faith has been further bolstered by educators' misguided attempts to categorize management as a science. This trend gained popular-ity in the 1960s, when business faculties embarked on a quest for greater respectability within universities where peers often viewed their programs as trade schools which, in the words of one contemporaneous account, were relegated to the "foot of the academic table."[19] In the hunt for greater prestige, they turned increasingly to quantitative analysis and the methods of social science to develop the burgeoning theories that now de-fine every business discipline.

This has served scholars well, for business schools are flour-ishing and enjoying much greater respect, funding, and influ-ence. However, the societal effects of management science are another matter. Unlike the descriptive and explanatory theories of the natural sciences, the pseudo-scientific theories of busi-ness do more than describe and explain — they actually shape business behaviors and values.

As Ghoshal sees it, "a precondition for making business stud-ies a science has been the denial of any moral or ethical consid-erations in our theories and, therefore, in our prescriptions for management practice."[20] This denial is implicit in the insistence by many business professors and executives that all decisions must be justified by a utilitarian "business case" showing direct benefit to the bottom line. This was brought home to me by a former colleague, a finance professor, who harrumphed in an e-mail that teaching ethical responsibility in business is "a lot of

19. Robert Gordon and James Edwin Howell, *Higher Education for Busi-ness* (New York: Columbia University Press, 1959), p. 4.

20. Ghoshal, "Bad Management Theories Are Destroying Good Manage-ment Practices," p. 77.

fluff and feel-good stuff without any economic justification!" In his view, the rightness or wrongness of behaviors can be measured only in dollars and cents. Researchers Mitroff and Denton have heard similar objections and flatly conclude that any association with non-scientific logic is "the literal kiss of death in the academic world." Many faculty thus accept that spiritual considerations "should be addressed outside of work, and definitely outside of traditional scholarship."[21]

What a contrast with Bob, the CEO who didn't wait for a cost-benefit analysis before deciding to devote time and money to the care of employees losing their jobs. With the theologian Reinhold Niebuhr, he understood that an over-reliance on scientific criteria in human relationships diminishes our dependence on God and our concern for others:

> The relation between "I and Thou" is not a scientific but an existential procedure. The turning of the self from itself as the center of life to God and the neighbor is also not scientific. The correlation of historic facts requires imagination, wisdom, and humility, which are not properly defined as "scientific." These attitudes require existential commitments, denials of self-interest, and recognition of the finiteness of all human knowledge. . . . If we fully analyze these characteristically human elements in history, we will not only cease to worship so uncritically at the altar of science. We will be less apologetic for the essence of a religion of history and revelation.[22]

We will return to this issue in Chapter Four as we look more closely at the Christian's quest for authenticity in a world where weekday occupations define so much of our identity, self-understanding, and engagement with others. But first let us turn to the world of the church to explore its part in separating faith from work.

21. Mitroff and Denton, *A Spiritual Audit of Corporate America*, p. 17.

22. Reinhold Niebuhr, "The Tyranny of Science," *Theology Today* 10, no. 4 (January 1954): 471.

Questions to Consider

- Why does it often seem difficult to live out the Christian imperative to love one's neighbor in the context of our daily work?
- How might employers appropriately accommodate religious expression and practice in the workplace? What are some practical examples?
- What are the spiritual and psychological consequences for Christians who fail to reconcile faith life and work life?

CHAPTER TWO

The World of Church

We have seen that today's business culture can be an obstacle for Christians seeking to bring faith to work. But the people we interviewed had often found it just as hard to bring their work-related concerns to church. "There is such a disconnect," said a chamber-of-commerce executive who confided that his work leaves him "spiritually dead" despite his active involvement in church. A director of a large charitable organization summed up a common sentiment: "I think the church provides a solid foundation for faithful living, but I'm not sure the connection is made to work. It's much easier to talk about living out your faith through volunteerism, community engagement, or financial giving than to talk about a faithful approach to work issues." Some said the church intentionally avoids such issues:

> "Many of us go to church as a respite from our weekday stress. Business isn't something people really want brought up at church."
>
> "Church is a place to get spiritually centered. I'm not sure it wants a role in workplace matters."
>
> "It would be important to feel the freedom to talk about work-related problems with my pastor, but for some reason it seems it wouldn't be appropriate."
>
> "The church expects us to handle those situations personally."

As noted earlier, a scant few of our respondents were inclined to seek work-related guidance from members of clergy. It may not be surprising, then, that the ministers conducting these interviews found them eye-opening and a bit humbling, especially when their own parishioners said they doubted if a pastor could possibly grasp their problems at work:

> "I think preachers spend a lot of time, and rightly so, thinking about ancient problems. And while I'm sure people in Bible times wrestled with tough problems, our world is very different from theirs."
>
> "Clergy are perceived solely as spiritual advisers; they are placed on a pedestal and not seen as advisers to business-people."
>
> "To [seek a pastor's advice] would presume that the minister had some specific knowledge of business, [of] the issues involved in a particular situation, and of likely consequences for short- and long-term profits."
>
> "The minister is not in tune with today's workplace and could not relate . . . so it would be better to talk with someone who would automatically understand without getting me frustrated."

Our researchers discovered a widely held perception of clergy as disinterested in church members' work lives. The disappointed pastor of a small-town congregation said, "I would have thought those active in our church would have said the church was helpful in their business life in dealing with ethical and moral questions." But they didn't. A business owner who faced an ethical quandary over tax payments echoed the views of many: "I did not approach the church because ethical issues in business are not of interest to any preacher I know. There is more of an emphasis on your family and how you live your personal life." Another said, "My pastor has no idea what I do for a living, and has never shown any interest in finding out by starting a conversation on the subject. He knows a great deal about my family, though."

These interviews were the first serious conversations most of these ministers had initiated with laypeople about the realities of work life. Not coincidentally, the conversations were also a new experience for most church members. "This [interview] is the first time a preacher has ever asked me anything about my career," one said. "Do we just have the idea we aren't supposed to talk much about this stuff at church?"

What's more, no respondent could recall a sermon or lesson at church that specifically addressed business or workplace issues, though several cited teachings on more general topics (e.g., love, forgiveness, tolerance) that could apply in a variety of social situations. A corporate executive described her pastor's sermons as offering "generally useful wisdom, but never any examples to connect it to the workplace." An earlier study by Doug Sherman and William Hendricks yielded a similar finding. In a survey of 2,000 people who regularly attend church, 90 percent responded "no" to the question "Have you ever in your life heard a sermon, read a book, listened to a tape, or been to a seminar that applied biblical principles to everyday work issues?" Sherman and Hendricks conclude, "The church has grown virtually silent on the subject of work."[1]

This is not to suggest that parishioners do not find ways to apply Christian teachings in their work, for studies show that many do; but they usually find that such connections must be made without much help from the church. Robert Wuthnow believes that clergy have been "reluctant to draw close connections, fearing that they did not themselves understand what people did during the work week or feeling that work was a kind of neutral zone."[2]

As one of our pastor-interviewers put it, "Ethical and moral issues seem to abound within the business community, both profit and non-profit, and the overwhelming conclusion is that

1. Doug Sherman and William Hendricks, *Your Work Matters to God* (Colorado Springs: NavPress, 1987), p. 16.
2. Robert Wuthnow, *God and Mammon in America* (New York: Free Press, 1994), p. 54.

the church is not addressing these concerns. But the reason why is still a difficult question to answer." Difficult, yes, but the question has begun to capture the attention of a variety of writers and researchers like Edward R. Dayton, who observes, "Few churches appreciate their business people as a window on the world, and fewer still provide business people with opportunities to discuss in depth the integration of business and Christian values."[3]

A study by Laura Nash and Scotty McLennan finds that many Christians are "looking for ways to live their Christian beliefs and values at work, as they do at home and at church. . . . [Yet] even deeply faithful Christians in business tend to feel a strong disconnect between their experience of the church or private faith, and the spirit-challenging conditions of the workplace."[4] And David A. Krueger adds, "For some people religious life and business practice are integrally related in a creative tension. For others — both clergy and business professionals — the worlds of church and corporate life are galaxies apart, separated by ignorance, hostility, apathy, language, interests, values."[5]

Too often the implicit message from the church, just as from business, is that Christians might as well learn to accept that faith simply cannot be made relevant to work life and should therefore be kept in the private domain. In fact, many people have done just that. Although most of our interviewees agreed that the church should do more to bridge faith and work, quite a few were ambivalent about mixing workday worries with their Sunday respite. Some of them had long abandoned any notion of coherence and had effectively compartmentalized their lives by relegating their weekday work to what Helmut Thielicke calls "a

3. Edward R. Dayton, *Succeeding in Business without Losing Your Faith* (Grand Rapids: Baker Book House, 1992), pp. 123-24.

4. Laura Nash and Scotty McLennan, *Church on Sunday, Work on Monday: The Challenge of Fusing Christian Values with Business Life* (San Francisco: Jossey-Bass, 2001), p. 5.

5. David A. Krueger, "Connecting Ministry with the Corporate World," in *On Moral Business*, ed. Max L. Stackhouse et al. (Grand Rapids: Wm. B. Eerdmans, 1995), p. 882.

temporal sphere in which the radical commandments of the Sermon on the Mount do not seem to apply, a sphere which consequently cannot be called into question."[6]

Distorted Doctrine

We are seeing that these two spheres of life are kept apart by powerful centrifugal forces. In the church these forces are fueled by history and sustained by the false dichotomies of sacred and secular, eternal and temporal, public and private.

Sacred and Secular

Anyone who has spent much time in the church is likely aware of its hierarchy of occupations. (See Figure 2.1.) At the peak of the pyramid are full-time clergy and missionaries, followed closely by other paid workers in Christian ministry. Their jobs are seen as genuine *callings*, often validated by special ceremonies and rituals. Just below them in rank are the so-called helping professions — social workers, nurses, and the like — whose work aligns neatly with the church's ministry priorities. Moving further down the pyramid we find the vast majority of Christians — salespeople, postal workers, accountants, business owners, electricians, corporate executives, lawyers, and countless others who comprise most of the body of Christ. Seldom are their jobs described as callings or celebrated by the church. We interviewed a high school teacher who astutely summed up the harm done by a caste system that devalues much good and necessary work:

> I don't think many people understand how a sense of vocation applies to their work, especially if they are not in a ministerial or helping profession. It's clear to me, since I'm a teacher, but

6. Helmut Thielicke, *Theological Ethics*, vol. 1, ed. William H. Lazareth (Philadelphia: Fortress Press, 1966), p. 364.

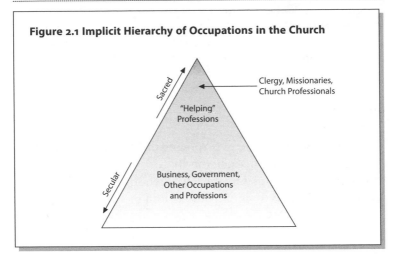

Figure 2.1 Implicit Hierarchy of Occupations in the Church

how do accountants know their work can be pleasing to or glorify God? How do attorneys hear the Holy Spirit in contentious cases? How can retail managers exhibit the love of Christ?

I was astonished recently to hear this hierarchy colorfully depicted in a sermon by a well-loved, retired minister. He declared that the church is like a circus that requires all kinds of workers — some to pitch the tent, some to take tickets, and even some to clean up after the elephants. At first he seemed to be working toward a rather strained metaphor for Romans 12:4-5 ("Just as each of us has one body with many members, and these members do not all have the same function, so in Christ we who are many form one body, and each member belongs to all the others").[7] But soon it was clear that his vision of the body of Christ was much more hierarchical than anything the apostle Paul ever imagined. He explained that the responsibility of everyone in the church, as in the circus, is to support the *performers*, chief among whom is the preacher in the pulpit. Granted, his imagery was a bit unusual, but the message that clergy are the stars of the

7. Unless otherwise noted, biblical texts are from the *New International Version* (Grand Rapids: Zondervan Bible Publishers, 1985).

show is quite common indeed. Consider these words of an earnest, freshly ordained seminary graduate preaching to a downtown Atlanta congregation with many businesspeople:

> Generations of people in this country find their identity in their jobs. But that is an empty life, a life that leads you down a path of nothingness. But what might it mean if God says, "Now you are the one to go deliver the message." Your life must be interrupted if you are to be an instrument in meeting the world's needs. You must be ready to respond to the calling that God has on your life. Think about the untouchables in India. What if God said, "I want you to be the one to travel over there and give them the message?" What about the epidemic of AIDS in Africa? What if God is calling you to go do something about it?

Must we really go to India or Africa to be instrumental in meeting the world's needs? Could it be that God also needs Christians to serve the world as factory workers, hairstylists, and bond traders?

These two ministers at opposite ends of their careers had the best of intentions, but I doubt if either had ever considered the disastrous consequences — for the church or for individual believers — of a theology that elevates an ecclesiastical elite while subtly devaluing the rest of the body. It is an attitude that betrays a distorted conception of Christian vocation and calling, one that sorts human activities into contrived categories of secular and sacred, suggesting that God is more concerned with church-sponsored work than with Christians being faithful in a thousand other daily contexts.

We should ask ourselves what is being communicated when a church allots time on Sunday morning to commission a short-term mission team for ten days in Mexico, yet does nothing to commission new college graduates for their careers in business or government or education. The crippling and unambiguous message is that ten days of volunteer work are more important to the church — and, by implication, to God — than a Christian's lifelong occupation.

Surely many of us have experienced doubts about the value of our own work. Pastors, too, have days of doubt. But let's be honest; it is much easier to find meaning in some jobs than in others.

I am reminded of a pastor who told me of a woman who suffered bouts of depression and marital strife. "She never smiled — always seemed bitter." He had counseled her on several occasions, but he never fully understood her situation until one afternoon when he stopped to see her at the poultry-processing plant where she was employed. Her shift was just ending, and she showed him the production line where she had just stood for eight hours gutting chickens with a knife. "Her work was grueling, messy, and smelly," he recalled, "and I realized at once why she had so little joy in her life." It is hard to find much redemptive value in repetitively cutting chickens or in hundreds of other jobs that must be contrary to the Creator's intention for human flourishing. There are well-paid lawyers and executives, too, who find it hard to see any divine purpose in their life-draining work.

By and large, the church is ill-prepared for the woman who wonders what Sunday worship has to do with her hard hours at the chicken factory. The tendency to devalue "secular" work only makes it more difficult to look to the faith community for support, encouragement, or constructive guidance. The writer of Ecclesiastes poignantly captures this sense of despair: "So what do people get in this life for all their hard work and anxiety? Their days of labor are filled with pain and grief; even at night their minds cannot rest. It is all meaningless" (Eccles. 2:22-23, NLT). We will return to this problem in Chapter Five as we investigate the concept of Christian vocation.

Finding meaning in work is an ancient problem for believers, as is the tendency to divide life into secular and sacred categories. Members of the early church were familiar with Greco-Roman philosophy and its tendency to bifurcate human beings into mind and body. For Aristotle and his successors, the body was prone to evil and existed for base, utilitarian functions, while the mind had the potential for reason and the apprehension of truth, beauty, and justice. Thus, the *Vida Contemplativa* (life of contemplation) was elevated above the *Vida Activa* (life of work and physical activity), leading to a social hierarchy where the intellectual elite were supported by craftsmen, merchants, and manual laborers.

Certainly this philosophy influenced the first Christians and their contemporaries; however, even the leaders of the earliest church had "real world" jobs to support themselves and the nascent Christian movement: Paul was a tentmaker, Lydia a merchant, and Peter a fisherman, among many examples. Jesus worked as a carpenter. It was common in this period for Jewish rabbis to earn their living as craftsmen, merchants, or farmers.

Very little social or occupational hierarchy is evident in the New Testament church, where diverse functions within the group were thought to be equally valuable to God. "There is neither Jew nor Greek, slave nor free, male nor female, for you are all one in Christ Jesus" (Gal. 3:28). Inevitably the church evolved into a more established institution, and egalitarian values gave way to formal structures that increasingly placed ministerial responsibility and authority in the hands of local bishops. "By the third century, the clergy/laity gap widened to the point of no return," according to Frank Viola and George Barna. They add with a note of sarcasm, "Clergymen were the trained leaders of the church — the guardians of orthodoxy — the rulers and teachers of the people. They possessed gifts and graces not available to lesser mortals."[8]

The writings of the Church Fathers during this period began to echo earlier Greco-Roman philosophy by placing sacred occupations above secular ones. The influential bishop of Caesarea, Eusebius, wrote in the fourth century,

> Two ways of life were thus given by the Lord to his church. The one is above nature and beyond common human living; it admits not marriage, child-bearing, property, nor the possession of wealth. . . . Like some celestial beings, these gaze down upon

8. Frank Viola and George Barna, *Pagan Christianity? Exploring the Roots of Our Church Practices* (Carol Stream, Ill.: BarnaBooks/Tyndale House Publishers, 2008), pp. 122-23.

human life, performing the duty of a priesthood to Almighty God for the whole race. . . .

And the more humble, more human way prompts men to join in pure nuptials, and to produce children, to undertake government, to give orders to soldiers fighting for right; it allows them to have minds for farming, for trade, and for the other more secular interests as well as religion.[9]

At about this time, the Roman emperor Constantine embraced the Christian faith and granted church leaders great political and economic influence, further elevating their jobs above those of the masses. For several hundred years thereafter, the early ideal of a community of equals was kept alive and modeled only within some of the monastic orders, such as the Benedictines. By the High Middle Ages, theologians had formulated a dualistic doctrine of work. Thomas Aquinas in the thirteenth century molded his systematic Christian theology to the contours of Aristotle's ideas, where the life of the mind represented the height of human fulfillment. It was a theology that affirmed the clergy as stewards of higher knowledge, rightly belonging to a world apart: the realm of the sacred.

Against this medieval backdrop the theologian and former monk Martin Luther challenged church authority and sought to restore a New Testament ideal of human beings serving God's kingdom through a variety of practical and equal occupations. (At the time this was seen as moving the church toward the *profane*, a Latin word meaning "outside the temple.") For Luther, work represented an avenue for loving and serving both neighbor and God. With John Calvin and other Reformers, he led a movement to replace the Roman Catholic hierarchy with a "priesthood of all believers." The Reformers' insistence that individuals need not rely on clergy to mediate their personal relationships with God became a basic tenet of Protestantism. Calvin taught that gifts are dispersed by God among all believers in

9. Quoted in Peter Robert Lamont Brown, *The Body and Society* (New York: Columbia University Press, 1988), p. 205.

order to equip the body of Christ for service in every area of life. It was a concept with the potential to ennoble Christians' work in everyday contexts.

These teachings notwithstanding, the emergent Protestant church continued to treat paid clergy as the *real* priesthood and held fast to an implied doctrine of work defined by a secular-sacred dualism. Even as the Reformers themselves propounded a more democratic theology of the laity, they saw preaching and the administration of the sacraments by ordained clergy as the centerpieces of Christian life and worship, insisting that the high calling to full-time ministry was of greater value than other occupations in the kingdom of God. Yes, Christians could be used by God in work outside the church, but this was of secondary importance. Such was the rationale for the hierarchy that is perpetuated by today's church.

By the time of the Enlightenment, the secularism of the Renaissance had already begun to erode the church's social and political clout. Theology was losing its traditional place as "queen of the sciences," as rationalism eclipsed divine revelation as the recognized source of truth. The cultural soil was being tilled for concepts like *management science* eventually to take root. Enlightenment utilitarianism promoted a pragmatic work ethic, supplanting the older idea that work has value only insofar as it serves God and neighbor.

In the worldview of modernity, which persists in our time, work is performed with little sense of serving God. All too often it is just something to be endured — a means to other ends, such as paying the rent, feeding the family, and supporting the church (which in turn hires people to do God's work on our behalf).

Eternal and Temporal

The early church's perspective on many things, including work, was quite different from our own, for believers lived each day expecting the imminent return of Jesus Christ. This eschatology had profound implications for practical theology, as God was surely on the verge of bringing a cataclysmic end to the present age and ushering in a new era. The earth was but a temporary stage for the final scene in the great drama of God's relationship with humanity. Understandably, the church busied itself with the salvation of humankind in obedience to Christ's Great Commission to make disciples of all nations. It is easy to imagine how the work of an architect, a farmer, or a merchant may have seemed less important.

For the first three centuries, the promised kingdom of God was mostly understood to be an eternal and spiritual realm not of the temporal world. It was Augustine in the fourth century who popularized a different interpretation — that the church is called to make visible the kingdom of God on earth. Over time the church gained enthusiasm for earthly ministries of service, but a powerful theological thrust continued to push for the primacy of other-worldly priorities.

Even today, especially in evangelical and pietistic traditions, believers are exhorted to keep their eyes on the eternal, for the things of this earth will not last. While it is undeniable that the "grass withers and the flowers fall" (Isa. 40:7), an inordinate emphasis on soteriology (salvation) can lead to an individualistic understanding of one's relationship with God, diminishing the Christian's larger responsibilities for the created world and those who inhabit it.

This emphasis is evident in preaching, teaching, and popular books that speak of the workplace solely as a mission field for evangelism. Often overlooked in such messages is the fact that the Great Commission is not limited to leading others to eternal salvation: "Therefore go and make disciples of all nations, baptizing them in the name of the Father and of the Son and of the Holy Spirit, and teaching them to obey everything I have commanded you . . ." (Matt. 28:19-20). Of all of the things Christ commanded, most can be summarized as love of God and neighbor — observing the Golden Rule, caring for the sick, feeding the hungry, clothing the poor, praying for enemies, and so on. One would be hard-pressed to find in Christ's teachings a rationale for an other-worldly faith that fails to take seriously one's life and work in this world. What's more, an artificial separation of eternal and temporal devalues the *first* great commission, found in the Genesis narrative, where God instructs humans to tend and care for creation — real work that is at once both temporal and sacred.

I find it interesting that the great spiritual leaders in human history are admired largely because they have managed to overcome the temporal and mundane to discover a deeper sense of the eternal and universal. We often think of spiritual disciplines as those habits that lift our consciousness above the daily rat race. While it is true that prayer and meditation are essential to the Christian life, these are not means of escaping reality; rather, they are to strengthen us so that we may lean ever harder into the reality of the here and now.

Public and Private

In the last chapter we considered Albert Carr's warning that trying to bring faith to work leads to unhealthy stress. What, then, is the church's advice to those struggling to make this connection? Often it is not too different from Carr's. I recently heard a Scottish pastor describe how his church ministers to people who work in the nearby business district. "Our doors are open every weekday to anyone seeking a place of prayer, reflection, and solitude." He explained that the church should be a "place of Sabbath," a quiet escape for the work-weary. To be sure, such a place meets a real need in today's hyper-busy society, for Christ himself invites us to unburden ourselves and take rest in him. But shouldn't the church also emulate the Christ who calls us to the difficult task of making the good news of the gospel real to the world, including the workplace?

Too often the church portrays itself as a place of refuge rather than a spiritual gymnasium to strengthen Christians for the transformative work they must do in the world. "To belong to the church is not just to belong to a community of believers who come together to 'get something out of' a church service, to be 'fed' and 'blessed,'" writes Shirley Guthrie. "It is to belong to a community of people who come together to be renewed so that they can go back into the world to serve God as they serve their fellowmen."[10] With active church members spending less than 2 percent of their waking hours at church, how much time is devoted to equipping them for their own public ministries?

The church's preoccupation with the private sphere of life is evident in many ways. Think of the litany of illnesses, deaths, and births in church newsletters and Sunday-morning prayers, reminding us weekly of what must surely matter most to God. Many of the people we interviewed shared a perception that the church is unconcerned about their lives in the public sphere:

> "The church rarely addresses [work-related] issues. It seems to be more directed toward individual relationships with Christ."
>
> "I do not think it is an interest of the church to help one resolve work problems."
>
> "Family issues, drug and alcohol problems, crises of faith are concerns for my pastor. . . . It is hard for me to waste the time of one faced with life issues on a personal business issue. I've never heard anything to the contrary at any event I have attended at my church."
>
> "Pastors are too busy taking care of the sick and dying to get involved in people's work whims and troubles."

Is faith only of value when healing is needed? Is it not essential to living our daily lives as instruments of God's healing power in the world? Church culture, like business culture, reinforces the notion that the proper place for faith is the private sphere. Despite this, many men and women in the pews are not easily persuaded that the God they worship on Sunday morning is unconcerned with how they make their living.

---

10. Shirley Guthrie, *Christian Doctrine* (Atlanta: John Knox Press, 1968), pp. 333-34.

The Influence of Theological Education

Those who perceive pastors as indifferent to their weekday work may wonder why this is so often the case. An explanation may be found in the educational institutions that prepare men and women for church ministry and define their future jobs and priorities. Nash and McLennan surveyed 154 seminary students at 14 diverse institutions to explore how future pastors are being prepared "to minister to members of the business community."

> When we probed for a particularized connection between faith and work, the response showed little depth or experience. When asked what business books or journals they studied, very few had any experience at all. When asked, "Have you discussed or been given any scripture passages to study with the explicit purpose of understanding God's message with respect to business or the responsibilities of the businesspeople?" respondents offered a range of passages that tended toward portraying bad business behavior.[11]

These findings are consistent with a recent review of courses offered by eighteen leading theological seminaries and divinity schools in the United States.[12] Only a few electives at a handful of the schools are described as addressing vocational or work-related issues. Several more focus on broader economic topics, such as social justice for the poor. Yet these institutions collectively offer dozens of courses on marriage, family, children,

11. Nash and McLennan, *Church on Sunday, Work on Monday*, p. 163.
12. The author reviewed the 2008-09 course catalogs, course descriptions, and degree requirements at Asbury Theological Seminary, Boston University School of Theology, Chicago Theological Seminary, Columbia Theological Seminary, Dallas Theological Seminary, Denver Theological Seminary, Duke Divinity School, Fuller Theological Seminary, Graduate Theological Union, Harvard Divinity School, Howard University School of Divinity, McCormick Theological Seminary, Princeton Theological Seminary, University of Chicago Divinity School, University of Notre Dame Department of Theology, Vanderbilt Divinity School, Wake Forest School of Divinity, and Yale Divinity School.

death, hospital visitation, psychological counseling, and other topics most relevant to the private sphere. The message of these curricula is clear about where pastors and priests — and, by extension, the church itself — should spend the most time and energy. A traditional theological education provides a foundation for ministry in diverse contexts, but the typical seminary experience is unlikely to inspire ministries that equip business and professional people for faithful service in public life.

"The church should acknowledge that its most visible spokespersons, the clergy, are, generally speaking, very poorly trained to intervene on economic and business matters," writes business ethicist Gedeon Josua Rossouw. "Most theological training grossly neglects a theological perspective on business and economics."[13] This neglect is also apparent in theological scholarship, as surprisingly little published research is relevant to economic life at the micro (individual) or meso (organizational) levels. Theological scholars have shown considerably greater interest in macro critiques of the economic system.

Still another challenge for theological education is that many students arrive for their first day of class with negative perceptions of business and professional life outside of the church. It is common for today's students at divinity schools and theological seminaries to be preparing for their second or third careers. According to one report, second-career students comprise more than half of the U.S. seminary student population.[14] Although it would seem that prior experience as a salesperson or a lawyer might predispose a ministry student to seek relevant connections between his or her past and future careers, I have found that a great many career-changers at the seminary are all too eager to leave their past behind. Very often they tell of disappointing experiences or even failures in earlier jobs, and many are looking to ministry as a "higher calling" and more satisfying career.

13. Gedeon Josua Rossouw, "Business Ethics: Where Have All the Christians Gone?" *Journal of Business Ethics* 13 (1994): 565.

14. Carnegie Samuel Calian, *The Ideal Seminary: Pursuing Excellence in Theological Education* (Louisville: Westminster John Knox Press, 2002), p. 59.

In his critique of seminary education, Carnegie Samuel Calian asks, "What unique knowledge and skills are acquired from the seminary that can address the dehumanizing forces and temptations of the marketplace? Many people view seminaries as largely irrelevant to the realities of survival in a harsh and unforgiving society."[15] To be fair, we must note that concerns about practical relevance have been debated since the first American theological seminaries were established more than two hundred years ago, designing postgraduate programs that continue to be the model for most of today's institutions. A three-year curriculum in Bible, theology, church history, and practical theology cannot cover every topic that interests faculty or students. Earlier seminaries provided an education heavily weighted toward ancient languages and theory, followed by a practical apprenticeship. Today's graduates are expected to emerge ready to preach, teach, counsel, manage, fund-raise, and lead, though much of their academic training has necessarily been devoted to scholarship in essential subjects of somewhat less practicality.

It would be unrealistic to expect many theological institutions to add new courses in applied ministry to their Master of Divinity curricula. Fortunately, this may not be necessary. Much can be accomplished within existing courses by more intentionally connecting the dots between theology and the public lives of Christians. It is beyond the scope of this book to propose specific curriculum revisions, but it must be stressed that virtually all of the academic disciplines are rich with opportunities to bridge this gap.

Meanwhile, immediate and even greater opportunities exist in continuing education classes for pastors, and in Doctor of Ministry programs that serve clergy who are already employed in parish ministry and other settings. Here again, a review of course offerings at leading seminaries and divinity schools found very few opportunities for working pastors to hone their knowledge and skills for ministry with businesspeople. Among

15. Calian, *The Ideal Seminary,* pp. 48-49.

these exceptions were several elective courses at Columbia Theological Seminary, including the doctoral seminar where students conducted the research discussed in these pages.

The Business of the Church

Most parish ministers have managerial responsibilities, such as budgeting, hiring, supervising, and purchasing, though it seems many church members either do not understand this or harbor doubts about pastors' competence in these roles. When our interviewees were asked why they had not sought pastoral counsel about work-related matters, quite a few shared misgivings about the church's own management:

> "How well does the church conduct its business affairs? Would any of their practices be relevant for the world?"
> "The church is not a good example itself. Consequently, church officers burn out or become too attached to their responsibilities."
> "The church's support comes from businesspeople, but we are not always confident the church manages that money responsibly."
> "I see all the same problems in the church working environment."

Of course, the church is a business, and a sizable one at that. Taken as a whole, churches and other places of worship continue to receive the largest share of Americans' charitable giving, more than education, human services, health, and other categories. Two-thirds of all adults, and 76 percent of Protestants, make such contributions. Annual per-capita giving by Protestants averaged $1,304 in 2004.[16] Total annual giving to religious congre-

---

16. "Americans Donate Billions to Charity, But Giving to Churches Has Declined," *The Barna Update*, 24 April 2005, accessed online at www.barna.org.

gations in the U.S. exceeds $80 billion,[17] a figure that translates to a like amount of spending and investment.

Dollar totals notwithstanding, it has never been popular to speak of the church as a business, for many prefer to see the priorities of the church as sacred and eternal, not secular and temporal. As long ago as the mid-1960s, an editor of *Presbyterian Life* magazine observed, "The denomination seems to want to delude itself. The officials and its membership . . . share the fantasy that they are not an ecclesiastical business juggernaut."[18]

Whether or not we are comfortable with acknowledging it, business management is an indispensable facet of ministry. Churches hire and pay staff, own and manage property, invest money, keep accounting records, file financial reports with government agencies, hire management and fund-raising consultants, comply with employment laws, own fleets of vehicles, purchase goods and services, and advertise their own services to the marketplace. Larger churches frequently hire business managers supervised by clergy. Some churches own broadcast facilities, recreational complexes, day schools, night shelters, and medical facilities. Others even run profit-making businesses, including commercial rental properties, retail stores, food-service establishments, and even gambling enterprises. One megachurch (a term for those with more than two thousand members) reportedly earned $17 million selling consulting services to other churches.[19] More than a few churches and church leaders profit handsomely from book sales and musical recordings.

Managerial duties may weigh most heavily on pastors of smaller, less wealthy churches, where little staff support is available. These pastors also have the most at stake in fund-raising,

17. *America's Religious Congregations: Measuring Their Contribution to Society* (Washington, D.C.: Independent Sector, 2001), p. 4.

18. Quoted in Alfred Balk, *The Religion Business* (Richmond, Va.: John Knox Press, 1967), p. 27.

19. William Symonds et al., "Earthly Empires: How Evangelical Churches Are Borrowing from the Business Playbook," *BusinessWeek*, 23 May 2005, accessed online at http://www.businessweek.com/magazine/content/05_21/b3934001_mz001.htm.

as about one-third of the budget goes to the pastor's salary in the typical mainline congregation.[20] We should not be surprised, then, that church professionals face many of the same business challenges as other church members. "Clearly," write Nash and McLennan, "the church is as vulnerable to the problems of money as any other organization. Some of the most discordant events reported in our congregational interviews were over allocation of church funds."[21] Some estimates indicate that financial disagreements cause more church splits than do theological differences.

Even so, the church is reluctant to acknowledge its own ethical challenges related to financial misconduct and personnel management. In the last chapter we looked at how businesses and other organizations are beginning to address ethics and business conduct in a more intentional and professional manner. Some may think it ironic that the church has been much slower than business to focus on managerial ethics. Indeed, the suggestion that it should do so is often met with defensiveness and denial, as leaders reject the possibility of ethical shortcomings despite evidence that the more extreme cases of ecclesiastical crime now amount to as much as 15 percent of churches' income worldwide.[22]

I witnessed this resistance several years ago while serving on a task force to write a code of ethics for a major Protestant denomination. Unlike similar projects in the business context, where nearly everyone accepts that clear standards of conduct should be established and promoted, this project was made more difficult by leaders who insisted it was unnecessary. "Why would the church need a code of ethics?" asked a pastor in a focus group. "Isn't the Bible enough?" Yet the denomination's own

20. "Report Examines the State of Mainline Churches," press release, 7 December 2009, Barna Group, accessed online at http://www.barna.org/barna-update/article/17-leadership/323-report-examines-the-state-of-mainline-protestant-churches.

21. Nash and McLennan, *Church on Sunday, Work on Monday*, p. 178.

22. "Just What Is the Gospel?" *International Bulletin of Missionary Research* 30, no. 1 (January 2006): 28.

case logs made it clear that ethical failures involving money and business matters were all too common, fracturing trust, wrecking careers, and costing millions of dollars in legal fees and settlements.

John Calvin rightly observed that when we are "highly esteemed," it is easy to become "unduly credulous" about ourselves and defensive about any suggestion that we fail to measure up to expectations.[23] Similarly, Reinhold Niebuhr shows that spiritual pride and moral pride are powerful forces that cause organizations to blind themselves to their own shortcomings.[24]

Several studies of accounting in church organizations have actually found a pattern of resistance to management practices that are well-accepted by other businesses and not-for-profits. Peter Booth attributes this to a church culture, or "ideology," that de-emphasizes activities perceived as secular. He acknowledges that this tendency varies from church to church, but faults the influence of a "sacred-oriented" occupational group that is theologically trained but lacking in business acumen.[25] It would not be reasonable to expect theological seminaries to produce clergy who are also skilled business and financial managers. However, more could be done to develop these competencies through continuing education and lifelong learning resources.

If the church fails to meet the weekday needs of its members — and if it is uneasy about the management of its own business — this may be symptomatic of a larger theological struggle to make theological sense of economics. We turn now to an issue that has been debated in the church since the beginning: the problem of money.

23. John Calvin, *Institutes of the Christian Religion*, Book II, ed. John T. McNeill, trans. Ford Lewis Battles (Philadelphia: Westminster Press, 1975), p. 242.

24. Reinhold Niebuhr, *The Nature and Destiny of Man*, vol. 1 (New York: Charles Scribner's Sons, 1941), p. 204.

25. Peter Booth, "Accounting in Churches: A Research Framework and Agenda," *Accounting Auditing and Accountability Journal* 6, no. 4 (1993): 37-67.

Questions to Consider

- Do you agree that many pastors show little interest in the work lives of their parishioners?
- It is often said that the church should adopt better business practices. Why does "business thinking" sometimes feel out of place in the church?
- Do you agree that the church generally regards church-related work more highly than other occupations? If so, what may be done to flatten this hierarchy?

CHAPTER THREE

Uneasy Bedfellows: Money and the Church

The church's failure to bridge the gap between pew and workplace is deeply rooted in another issue: the Christian community's longstanding ambivalence about money. In today's society, work and money are so intertwined that we can hardly speak of one without the other. Money is not only a medium of exchange denoting the value of goods or services; it is a symbol of the value we assign to various types of work and, by extension, to those who perform the work. It is our generation's way of keeping score. The question "How much is she worth?" may inquire about an individual's wealth, but the answer almost certainly shapes our estimation of the person herself. Keeping up with the Joneses means more than having the latest car or party dress; it is about finding a place in the social hierarchy to validate one's self-worth.

"Money, being the principal means of organizing and ordering survival in the outer world, thus seems the most real thing in our lives," says the philosopher Jacob Needleman.[1] Even the church is thoroughly steeped in the money culture, for even there institutional success and individual status are measured with a financial yardstick. "How can we find a place to stand that is free from the influence of money so as to think impartially

1. Jacob Needleman, *Money and the Meaning of Life* (New York: Doubelday, 1991), p. 23.

45

about it and then plot our course according to deeper values?"[2] Can anything in our society be free from its influence? Money is a sensitive and intensely personal subject that we love to discuss in some circumstances, but dare not speak of in others.

Biblical Perspectives

In a memorable poem, Carl Sandburg describes money as power, freedom, a cushion, the root of all evil, the sum of blessings, "all of these — and more."[3] The Scriptures yield a similar amalgam of perspectives. On the one hand, we find biblical teachings that call us to give thanks for wealth as a gift and blessing from God. On the other, we are warned not to desire wealth and are even urged to renounce it altogether. This ambiguity, which accounts for the conflicting doctrinal understandings of money within today's church, exacerbates the Christian's difficulty in matters of remunerative work and vocation.

It is in the Old Testament where wealth is frequently treated as a gift or reward from God. There we find many accounts of nations and individuals prospering as a sign of divine favor. In Genesis, Abraham was blessed with great riches, and "Isaac planted crops in that land and the same year reaped a hundredfold, because the LORD blessed him. The man became rich, and his wealth continued to grow until he became very wealthy" (Gen. 26:12-13). Such stories are confirmed by teachings elsewhere: "The blessing of the LORD brings wealth, and he adds no trouble to it" (Prov. 10:22); "Humility and the fear of the LORD bring wealth and honor and life" (Prov. 22:4).

Yet material blessings are sometimes withheld from those who appear to be most obedient to God. In these cases, we are reminded that all wealth belongs to God, whose purposes we do not always understand. "The LORD sends poverty and wealth; he

2. Needleman, *Money and the Meaning of Life*, p. 159.
3. Carl Sandburg, "The People, Yes," *Rainbows Are Made* (New York: Houghton Mifflin, 1982), p. 41.

humbles and he exalts" (1 Sam. 2:7). Faithfulness is not a give-to-get formula for riches. In ancient times, just as today, prosperity comes to the just and unjust alike (Ps. 73:12-13).

If Scripture bears a consistent message about wealth, it is that the desire for it is never sanctioned. God permits some individuals to gain wealth, but the Old Testament is replete with warnings against desiring money or property for oneself. Abraham (then still called Abram) refuses the king of Sodom's offer of a lucrative reward for his services. "I have raised my hand to the LORD, God Most High, Creator of heaven and earth, and have taken an oath that I will accept nothing belonging to you, not even a thread or the thong of a sandal, so that you will never be able to say, 'I made Abram rich'" (Gen. 14:22-23). In renouncing this gift, Abraham shows that he can be content with what God chooses to give him. Solomon passes a similar test when he asks God for wisdom rather than wealth. God grants his request and adds, "Since you have asked for this and not for long life or wealth for yourself, . . . I will give you what you have not asked for — both riches and honor — so that in your lifetime you will have no equal among kings" (1 Kings 3:11-13).

Abraham's acknowledgment that his wealth comes from God is echoed throughout the Old Testament in the refrain that it is arrogant to take credit for one's own success. There is little room for the modern ideal of the "self-made" person. "You may say to yourself, 'My power and the strength of my hands have produced this wealth for me.' But remember the LORD your God, for it is he who gives you the ability to produce wealth. . . ." (Deut. 8:17-18). Other texts that emphasize being satisfied with one's possessions are summed up by the writer of Ecclesiastes (5:10): "Whoever loves money never has money enough; whoever loves wealth is never satisfied with his income. This too is meaningless."

More than meaningless, the desire for wealth is seen as an illusory and faithless quest for self-sufficiency and power. "The wealth of the rich is their fortified city; they imagine it an unscalable wall." By contrast, "The name of the LORD is a strong tower; the righteous run to it and are safe" (Prov. 18:11, 10). To avoid falling into this temptation, we are to pray for "neither poverty nor riches, but . . . only my daily bread. Otherwise, I may have too much and disown you and say, 'Who is the LORD?' Or I may become poor and steal, and so dishonor the name of my God" (Prov. 30:8-9). We may conclude that some money is necessary, but too much or too little is a spiritual danger. Jesus' disciples would have recognized this provocative proverb in what we now know as the Lord's Prayer. We have no difficulty asking for daily bread — but for daily bread *only?* How many of us today would sincerely pray for God *not* to make us rich?

Sharing with the poor was required by the earliest Hebrew laws. Landowners were not permitted to maximize their profits, for a percentage of the crops in their fields, orchards, or vineyards were to be left for those less fortunate. "When you reap the harvest of your land, do not reap to the very edges of your field or gather the gleanings of your harvest. Do not go over your vineyard a second time or pick up the grapes that have fallen. Leave them for the poor and the alien" (Lev. 19:9-10).

The major perspectives on money in the Old Testament may be summarized by three mutually dependent principles:

All wealth belongs to the sovereign God, whose purposes are not necessarily ours.

There is spiritual danger in seeking after money or property for oneself, as this turns us away from our proper dependence upon God.

Financial prosperity may indeed be a blessing, but a willingness to renounce wealth indicates that one is fit to be entrusted with it.

Turning to the New Testament, the biblical treatment of money becomes even more challenging for modern Christians. Here we find no indication that God is pleased to make us rich. Renunciation of wealth is demanded, and warnings about the *love* of money are even more pointed. "No one can serve two masters," Jesus declares in the Sermon on the Mount. "Either he will hate the one and love the other, or he will be devoted to the one and despise the other. You cannot serve both God and mammon" (Matt. 6:24). To love *mammon* — an Aramaic word meaning both money and wealth — is to *hate* God. Paul's letter to Timothy cautions that "the love of money is a root of all kinds of evil. Some people, eager for money, have wandered from the faith and pierced themselves with many griefs" (1 Tim. 6:10). Peter stresses that believers should be "not greedy for money, but eager to serve" (1 Peter 5:2). The writer to the Hebrews admonishes, "Keep your lives free from the love of money and be content with what you have, because God has said, 'Never will I leave you; never will I forsake you'" (Heb. 13:5). The recurring message is straightforward: Put your trust in God alone.

Throughout his public ministry Jesus speaks more about money than any other subject, including eternal salvation. In a poignant encounter chronicled by the three Synoptic Gospels, a wealthy young man asks the Messiah what he must do to be saved. Mark's account tells us that "Jesus looked at him and loved him," but instructed, "Go, sell everything you have and give to the poor, and you will have treasure in heaven. Then come, follow me." The man faced a stark choice between God and mammon, and "he went away sad, because he had great wealth" and could not bring himself to renounce it (Mark 10:21-24).

It is just at this moment that Jesus astonishes his companions (and all of us) by declaring, "It is easier for a camel to go through the eye of a needle than for a rich man to enter the kingdom of God" (Mark 10:25). Noteworthy in this story but often overlooked is how Jesus practices what he preaches by telling the man to give the money to the poor and *then* come follow him. By not asking him to give the money to his own ministry, Jesus performs an act of renunciation almost unimaginable in today's church.

The obligation to give to the poor is pervasive in Scripture, but Jesus takes this especially seriously. He sees money not as a neutral tool that we are free to use for good or for ill based on our priorities and values. Rather, mammon is a spiritual power that seeks to use *us* — a false deity that actually rivals God for our devotion. Nowhere does Jesus illustrate the power of money more powerfully than in a parable he tells in response to Peter's question about forgiveness (Matt. 18:21-35). A servant owes his master a large sum of money and is threatened with losing everything, including his family, because he cannot repay it. He pleads with his master, who shows mercy and forgives the debt, freeing the servant from financial bondage. Immediately thereafter, the servant encounters a fellow worker who owes him a small debt. Grabbing him by the throat, he demands repayment. Although just freed from his own indebtedness through the grace of his master, the servant shows that he is still captive to the insidious power of mammon and is unable to forgive others as he has been forgiven.

On another occasion, Jesus is speaking to a large crowd when a man calls out to him for help in resolving a conflict with his brother over how to divide their inheritance. Again, the teacher is less concerned with the problem at hand than with the dangerous power of mammon. "Watch out!" he warns. "Be on your guard against all kinds of greed; a man's life does not consist in the abundance of his possessions" (Luke 12:14). He goes on to remind that man that accumulated earthly wealth will be of no value to him when he dies.

New Testament teachings about money are very challenging indeed. Is it any wonder today's church fails to speak coherently on the subject? Should it surprise us when a businessperson feels torn between the drive to maximize profits and the biblical injunctions to forgive debts and to pray for neither poverty nor riches?

The Early Church: A Community of Sharing and Sacrifice

Such teachings were undoubtedly difficult for early Christians as well. There is little evidence that they were expected to renounce all possessions, for some in the New Testament had homes and ran businesses. But there was a remarkable spirit of sharing, as the bonds of community were strengthened by persecution and a zealous commitment to the gospel cause. The vivid picture emerging from the book of Acts is of a community devoted to mutual well-being. "All the believers were together and had everything in common. Selling their possessions and goods, they gave to anyone as he had need" (Acts 2:44-45). "All the believers were one in heart and mind. No one claimed that any of his possessions was his own, but they shared everything they had. . . . There were no needy persons among them. For from time to time those who owned lands or houses sold them, brought the money from the sales and put it at the apostles' feet, and it was distributed to anyone as he had need" (Acts 4:32, 34-35). John also stresses the New Testament imperative to share: "If anyone has material possessions and sees his brother in need but has no pity on him, how can the love of God be in him?" (1 John 3:17).

It is not possible to derive a clear doctrine of money from these texts, but we may conclude that the earliest Christians were expected to be selfless in support of one another and of the poor. Holmes Rolston describes their community as one where, "for a time at least, poverty was abolished. . . . And a world which had known very little of love or brotherhood was suddenly confronted with the spectacle of a brotherhood which went so deep that there was experienced on the basis of love a real sharing of wealth among the members of the church."[4] We also know that the church expected its members to be free from any desire for material wealth, as illustrated by the troubling story of Ananias and Sapphira, condemned for lying in order to appear more generous than they actually were (Acts 5:3-5).

The self-sufficiency of this first faith community did not last long, however, for the Jerusalem church began to disperse after Stephen's martyrdom amid rising persecution. In Paul's letters to newer congregations, we find him busily raising money for "the poor among the saints in Jerusalem" (Rom. 15:25-27; 1 Cor. 16:1-3; 2 Cor. 8-9). Even so, Paul does not advocate communal ownership of all property, but stresses that those who are capable of providing for their own families should not take unfair advan-

---

4. Holmes Rolston, *Stewardship in the New Testament Church* (Richmond, Va.: John Knox Press, 1946), p. 34.

tage of the generosity of others. He tells Timothy, "If anyone does not provide for his relatives, and especially for his immediate family, he has denied the faith and is worse than an unbeliever" (1 Tim. 5:8).

Predictably, money was a persistent theological problem for the maturing church as it expanded, challenging the dominant culture of the Roman Empire, but being shaped by it as well. The era from about 100 to 450, known as the Patristic period, was a crucial time for establishing many of the basic doctrines that continue to constitute Christian orthodoxy. Debates raged among church leaders over such essentials as the deity of Christ, the nature of the Trinity, the means of salvation, and the texts to be included in the canon of Scripture. Their conflicts were so rancorous that by the year 325 the emperor Constantine, who was then undergoing a gradual conversion to Christianity, convened a meeting of several hundred bishops to develop a consensus on key doctrinal questions.

Agreement on a doctrine of money, however, continued to be elusive. Long before the church was embraced by Constantine and the Roman elites, early Church Fathers tried to sort out a Christian view of money. Clement of Alexandria in the second century wrote extensively on the lifestyles of believers, concluding that the rich may receive salvation, but not without difficulty. He counseled a "rational" and temperate approach to the making and spending of money:

> For my part, I approve of Plato, who plainly lays it down as a law that a man is not to labour for wealth of gold or silver, nor to possess a useless vessel which is not for some necessary purpose. . . .
>
> But now love of money is found to be the stronghold of evil, which the apostle says "is the root of all evils, which, while some coveted, they have erred from the faith, and pierced themselves through with many sorrows."
>
> But the best riches is poverty of desires; and the true magnanimity is not to be proud of wealth, but to despise it. Boasting about one's plate is utterly base. For it is plainly wrong to care

much about what anyone who likes may buy from the market. But wisdom is not bought with coin of earth, nor is it sold in the market-place, but in heaven. And it is sold for true coin, the immortal Word, the regal gold.[5]

But church growth brought increasing numbers of wealthy members. By the middle of the third century, the church in the city of Rome was a well-organized institution, large enough to support about 1,500 poor people and to formalize the raising and spending of money. In 251 Bishop Cornelius's clergy numbered 155, and the church comprised a diverse cross-section of Roman society, including some well-to-do businesspeople. According to church historian Justo Gonzales, the "tradition persisted that riches were not objects of pride, and that their best use was to give them away." Those who held onto wealth may have exercised power in the church, but they "lost some of their prestige precisely because they had retained such wealth."[6]

In the early fourth century, around the time that Constantine's edict of Milan legalized Christianity and secured the church's ownership of property, an influential teacher named Lactantius was writing extensively about wealth and money in his *Divine Institutes*. While generally affirming the traditions of wealth renunciation and support of the poor, he contended that it is not realistic to expect *all* members of the church to give up their wealth. With the church now embraced by the emperor and the wealthy classes, he stopped short of calling for great sacrifices but instead counseled the rich to avoid excess and remember to help the poor.[7] He defended private property ownership, arguing that it is good for families and serves as a motivation to live responsibly.

Lactantius also introduced the notion that wealth is not a

5. *The Writings of Clement of Alexandria*, trans. William Wilson (Edinburgh: T&T Clark, 1967), pp. 212, 214.

6. Justo L. Gonzales, *Faith and Wealth: A History of Early Christian Ideas on the Origin, Significance, and Use of Money* (New York: Harper & Row, 1990), pp. 133-34.

7. Gonzales, *Faith and Wealth*, p. 136.

problem *per se,* but only when it is used irresponsibly — a rationale later to become common in church teachings. Indeed, some of his writings sound like modern-day stewardship sermons: Those who give generously may expect a blessing from God in return; what matters is not one's wealth, but one's attitude about it. This was a softening of the earlier teachings of Clement and of Cyprian of Carthage, who saw sacrificial giving as a spiritual discipline necessary to free one from enslavement to mammon. Of course, it must be remembered that the church of these earlier theologians comprised far fewer wealthy people.

So the church's doctrine of money evolved gradually to accommodate an increasingly upscale membership, especially after the momentous changes that occurred under Constantine. Throughout most of the fourth century, the church benefited from a close relationship with the political and economic powers of Rome, even to the extent that Roman officials throughout the empire were required to contribute financially to the church. The emperor paid to construct numerous churches, including the Basilica of Saint Peter in Rome, the impressive Church of the Apostles in Constantinople, and several major shrines in the Holy Land.

"When Constantine came to power, Christianity was mostly a religion of the middle and lower classes among the urban population," writes Gonzales, but before the end of the century, its members included some of the wealthiest Romans. New money, including substantial imperial contributions, led almost inevitably to corruption (such as the buying and selling of clergy ordination) and manipulation by political interests.[8] Within the Christian community these changes sparked counter-movements, especially in North Africa, where the asceticism and piety of monks in Egypt stood as a contrast to the church elsewhere, and where the Donatists accused church leaders of greed and capitulation to economic interests. This fight over the proper role of money in the church was one of the first of the great doctrinal battles plaguing the church

8. Gonzales, *Faith and Wealth,* p. 154.

through the centuries. It was also around this time that some clergy first began demanding money from Christians by construing Old Testament teachings on tithing to formulate a biblically questionable concept that persists today.

As the church gained power in the fourth century, the voices of noteworthy teachers and theologians continued to sound spirited warnings about the dangers of wealth. Basil of Caesarea, a wealthy man himself, spoke forcefully against usury and insisted that greed is the root cause of all poverty. Ambrose, bishop of Milan, declared as unjust nearly every means of making money (except agriculture) and equated underpaying workers with murdering them. John Chrysostom, bishop of Constantinople, taught that sharing wealth is the essence of Christian living, warning the rich that they have much more opportunity to sin than do the poor. He believed that Christians should keep for themselves only enough for subsistence.

Then, near the turn of the fifth century, Augustine of Hippo emerged as a seminal shaper of Christian theology and the most influential thinker since the New Testament writers. Like Clement and his other predecessors, the North African bishop sought to make a sharp distinction between needs and wants, teaching that material possessions should be strictly limited to those which enable us to sustain ourselves in the service of God. He promoted the by-then established tradition of giving to the poor as a means of atoning for one's own sin, and said that while Christ does not require everyone to give all they own to the poor, this is necessary for those who wish to be perfect in the eyes of God. In one treatise, he imagines Christ speaking of riches: "Do you love them? Send them on ahead [through almsgiving] where you can follow them; or else, when you are loving them on earth, you either lose them while you are alive or leave them behind when you are dead."[9] Today we might just say, "You can't take it with you."

9. Augustine, Sermon 345, *Works of Saint Augustine: A Translation for the Twenty-First Century*, trans. Edmund Hill, Part III — Sermons, vol. 10: Sermons 341-400 (New York: New City Press, 1995), p. 60.

Augustine struggled with economic issues, especially when theological principles became entangled with Roman law and custom. For example, he taught that it is a sin for lenders to charge interest on borrowed money — an almost universally held position of the church up until his time — but equivocated when poor debtors staged a rebellion to destroy the usurious letters of credit by which the rich exploited them. Augustine was indignant at this challenge to authority, condemning it as a crime.[10]

Taking the first four centuries as a whole, we find several recurrent themes in the church's theological discourses on money and wealth: (1) give generously, even sacrificially, to others; (2) recognize that God owns all things and intends them for the common good; (3) do not charge interest to borrowers, especially the poor; (4) recognize that wealth is not an evil, but the desire for it indicates a sinful heart and endangers the soul. (See Figure 3.1.)

Throughout history, as larger numbers of social, political, and economic elites joined the faith, the church's teachings became more accommodating of them. In his time, Augustine provided the same kind of accommodation, for no longer was the primary emphasis on the power of mammon as a danger to be renounced. The emerging consensus, which persists to this day in numerous forms, was that Christians should be detached emotionally, but not literally, from wealth — that riches are permissible for those who can keep their priorities straight and do their part to support the church (and presumably, through this, the poor).

The Middle Ages: Greater Accommodation of Wealth

By the fifth century, the Roman Empire was weakening, and the day was fast coming when encroaching northern tribes would sack Rome itself. Over the next thousand years, as smaller kingdoms emerged to rule sections of Europe and the lands surrounding the Mediterranean, the church was the sole unifying

10. Gonzales, *Faith and Wealth*, p. 221.

Figure 3.1. Classical Christian Teachings on Wealth

- Christians are required to give generously, even sacrificially, to ensure that the needs of others are met.

- Responsible ownership of private property is permissible, but all wealth is intended by God to be used for the good of all.

- It is wrong to charge interest on loaned money, and even more so if the borrower is poor.

- A desire for wealth indicates a sinful heart and endangers the soul.

---

force in the land, having amassed considerable power and wealth before the fall of the empire. Under its auspices, many of the scholastic, artistic, and scientific traditions of the ancient world were carried forward. The church developed into a multiform institution comprising diverse groups that often disagreed on theological questions about money and wealth.

Early in the medieval period, the personally wealthy Pope Gregory the Great continued and even expanded Augustine's accommodation of the rich. All but forgotten were the early church's calls for sacrificial generosity and warnings about the corrupting influence of mammon. Gregory's enormously influential *Book of Pastoral Rule* became a guide for bishops for hundreds of years. On the subject of money, it encourages preachers to craft their sermons in a manner that will not condemn the rich simply for being rich. Gregory offers a broader interpretation of Matthew 19:24, where Jesus compares a camel passing through the eye of a needle with a rich man trying to enter heaven. "Who does he mean by 'rich man' but any proud person . . . ?"[11] Elsewhere Gregory recommends comforting the poor with assurances that they "possess riches which they cannot

---

11. John Moorhead, *Gregory the Great,* The Early Church Fathers 14 (London and New York: Routledge and Taylor & Francis Group, 2005), p. 146.

see" and reminding the rich that "they can by no means hold onto the riches that they can see."

> . . . a rich person may be humble, or a poor person proud. And so the voice of the preacher ought to be adjusted to correspond to the life of the listener, so that he chastises the pride of the poor person with a strictness appropriate to the way in which it is not the poverty with which he has been afflicted which makes him bend over, and that he beguiles the humility of rich people with a gentleness appropriate to their not being lifted up by the abundance which supports them.[12]

The medieval church also relaxed traditional restrictions on money-lending, though most loans continued to be made by Jewish bankers who were permitted by their faith to lend money to non-Jewish merchants (but not to other Jews). Significantly, the church no longer regarded individual wealth as a sign of one's refusal to share with the needy. Responsibility for the poor was reduced to almsgiving, a penitential practice that conveniently provided forgiveness for the sin of avarice. This method of atoning for personal sins eventually developed into the complex, commercialized system of selling indulgences, so strongly condemned by the Protestant Reformers. (The excesses of *quid pro quo* donations to the church are summed up by the title of Jacques Le Goff's book, *Your Money or Your Life: Economy and Religion in the Middle Ages.*)

Over the centuries there were many variations of these teachings. In the thirteenth century, for instance, the Franciscan scholar John of Wales invoked much of Gregory's treatise on wealth, but took a slightly harder line on how it may be obtained. He condemned usury, fraud, and theft, as well as any desire to gain or hoard riches. Because it is impossible to be wealthy without loving wealth, he taught, the poor actually have an advantage.[13]

---

12. Moorhead, *Gregory the Great*, p. 97.

13. Jenny Swanson, *John of Wales: A Study of the Works and Ideas of a Thirteenth-Century Friar* (Cambridge: Cambridge University Press, 1989), p. 133.

His famous contemporary, Thomas Aquinas, concurred: "Poverty then is praiseworthy, inasmuch as it delivers a man from the vices in which some men are entangled by riches." He qualified this by saying that such an individual must be capable of using a simpler life to "give free attention to divine and spiritual things." With Aristotle, who profoundly influenced his theology, he saw contemplation as the noblest and best life. But he insisted that choosing poverty is "simply an evil" if it reduces "the good of riches, namely the helping of other people, and hinders self support" for no spiritual purpose.[14]

Like his medieval predecessors, Aquinas defended the ownership of private property and argued that it would be impractical to renounce all of one's possessions in order to help the poor, as this could only result in temporary help for a few. Even so, he expected Christians to use only what they truly needed to support themselves and their families. "Hence, whatever certain people have in superabundance is due, by natural law, to the purpose of succoring the poor."[15] For Aquinas, all goods, even those in private hands, should be used to meet the needs of all; like Aristotle, he considered this the rational thing to do. To this end, he approved of investing in businesses for financial returns, but insisted that profit-making should never be the prime motivation of the investor.

Aquinas maintained the church's long-standing prohibition against individuals charging interest on borrowed money. Yet the medieval church was itself a borrower and a lender, controlling a vast swath of the economy. It has been estimated that the church owned more than one-third of all the developed land in Europe before the year 900 and was likely the continent's leading employer.[16] By the thirteenth century, it was common practice

14. Thomas Aquinas, *Of God and His Creatures: An Annotated Translation of the Summa Contra Gentiles*, trans. Joseph Rickaby (Westminster, Md.: Carroll Press, 1950), p. 330.

15. Thomas Aquinas, *Summa Theologica*, vol. III, part II, second section (New York: Cosimo, 2007), p. 1474.

16. Robert Tollison et al., *Sacred Trust: The Medieval Church as an Economic Firm* (London: Oxford University Press, 1996), p. 9.

for the church to claim for itself the assets of deceased merchants or others accused of usury. Researchers have found that the papal treasury was "both a demander and a supplier of loans," with reports of interest-bearing loans from Italian bankers who were "pressing Pope IV for payment in 1262." The Vatican was "hard-nosed" with delinquent borrowers as it "quietly made usurious loans to its prelates (or forced them into such loans), while outwardly declaring public usurers anathema."[17]

Medieval teachings on money were limited almost exclusively to individual practice (micro-economics in today's terminology). It is fair to say that the church had not developed a theology capable of informing its own exercise of vast institutional and macro-economic responsibilities.

The Reformation: Rethinking Work and Its Monetary Rewards

Concern about the financial corruption of the church was a major impetus for the Protestant Reformation movement of the sixteenth century. Martin Luther, a former monk, famously challenged these failures in his "Disputation on the Power and Efficacy of Indulgences," better known today as his "95 Theses." While many issues converged to spark the Reformation, the selling of "indulgences" may have been the most catalytic and controversial. Under this system, members of the church were told that they could be exempted from God's punishment for certain sins, provided they paid money to support "good works" that could help earn their salvation. The scheme was a kind of insurance against eternal damnation. By the sixteenth century, indulgences were even sold to ensure forgiveness for people who had already died and were presumed to be in purgatory, awaiting final judgment. In Luther's view, the issue was not just the church's greed but its distortion of the doctrine of salvation, which he vehemently insisted is a free gift from God that cannot be bought with money or earned through good works.

17. Tollison et al., *Sacred Trust*, p. 118.

He and other Reformation leaders, especially John Calvin, were also concerned with adapting Christian doctrines to the economic realities of an expanding mercantile economy. No longer was wealth seen as a "zero-sum game" where one person's gain was another's loss. These theologians recognized that a growing economy could provide new financial opportunities for the poor, that almsgiving was not the only way to help them.

But even with this shift in thinking, the Reformers disapproved of the pursuit of personal riches. Calvin's sermon on the Eighth Commandment ("Do not steal") deals with the larger problem of money in the Christian life. Delivered in 1555 to citizens of the Genevan republic, where Calvin was the architect of a municipal government controlled by clergy, the sermon warned the wealthy that their oppression of the poor is tantamount to theft or even murder. Calvin continued, "Next is the matter of our not craving to be rich. For as soon as that lust for gain takes hold of us, it is certain that we will become thieves; it cannot be otherwise."[18] Luther also saw this danger, paraphrasing Proverbs 30:7-9: "Mammon has two properties: it makes us secure, first, when all goes well with us, and then we live without fear of God at all; secondly, when it goes ill with us, then we tempt God, fly from him, and seek after another God."[19]

Both of these Reformers taught that the proper attitude toward money is contentment with what God provides, a difficult thing for rich and poor alike. Challenging Aquinas and Aristotle, Luther contended that all work, even manual labor, has dignity and purpose as service to God. But he remained skeptical about commerce and urged people to accept their stations in life without striving for upward mobility (a vestige of the medieval feudal system).

Calvin agreed that all work can be service to God, but imbued the idea with more theological significance by teaching that an

18. John Calvin, *Sermons on the Ten Commandments*, ed. Benjamin W. Farley (Grand Rapids: Baker Books, 1980), p. 192.

19. Martin Luther, *The Table Talk of Martin Luther*, trans. William Hazlitt (London: H. G. Bohn, 1857), p. 66.

individual's worldly achievements may be a sign that he or she is among the elect — those chosen for eternal life. Thus, even the rich must work hard, for idleness is neglect of one's duty to serve God's kingdom through the continuing process of co-creation. Profits provide opportunities to expand one's service, especially through investments in worthy business ventures, but not to accumulate personal wealth or superfluous possessions. Accordingly, Calvin encouraged the active pursuit of money for investment purposes, a radical departure from earlier church edicts to give as much as possible to the poor. He believed that the poor could benefit from economic development, whereas too much charitable support might deprive them of the opportunity to work hard and to demonstrate that they are among the elect.

As Geneva became a hub for Protestants from all over Europe, Calvin's imprint on the Reformation led to lasting changes in Western thought about the value of work and the use of money. Today the so-called Protestant work ethic, which Max Weber attributes to Calvin, retains a powerful influence in our own society, where wealth is widely seen as the legitimate reward of hard work.

How much Calvin contributed to the rise of Western capitalism is debatable, for some rightly argue that he would not have condoned later forms of Calvinism that cleared the way for unbridled consumption. Yet he did create an opening for production-oriented capitalism and the private ownership of profit-making enterprises. Cameron Murchison explains,

> While it is true that certain [of Calvin's] theological claims sponsor habits and practices that can lead to capital accumulation — thus supporting production-oriented capitalism, other equally important theological claims sponsor habits and practices that tend to curb material acquisition due to the communal obligation to use excess wealth not for self-satisfaction but for needs of others — thus contending with a version of consumer-oriented capitalism that relentlessly attends only to consumer demand.
>
> Transposing all of this into an intentional practical theology of faithful living in economic matters brings us to some impor-

tant affirmations. God's creation and calling of people to productive, industrious lives, reflecting the image of the Creator in the creature, does undergird important economic values such as productivity and the co-generation of wealth. However, precisely because this doctrine of creation and calling has reference to the Creator, who has communal purposes for us as people who are necessarily yoked to our neighbors, productivity and wealth are not abstract, unfocused, and individualized — but concrete and aimed exactly at the construction of human community.[20]

Our Contemporary Confusion

It is certain that the economic legacy of the Reformation contributes to the ambivalent feeling of today's Christians seeking to relate their faith to their money-making activities. Jacob Needleman, who calls money the "battlefield of life," faults the Protestant Reformers for turning believers "toward the forces of life without providing adequate 'weapons' or precise knowledge of how to fight on that clamorous battlefield."[21] He is entirely right about this.

In the centuries following the Reformation, a convergence of social and economic forces gradually gave shape to the rationalism of the Enlightenment (thanks especially to the contributions of Scottish thinkers), which proclaimed the autonomy of the individual and gave rise to modern capitalism and liberal democracy. Enlightenment ideals placed the individual at the center of everything, with the freedom to pursue political, intellectual, and economic progress unhindered by either the church or monarchs. If individual freedom was to be limited at all, it could only be by rational consent in exchange for protection of individual rights, defined by John Locke as life, liberty, and property.

20. Cameron Murchison, "Reformed Resources for Practical Theology: The Christian Life and Consumer Capitalism," unpublished paper, 12 January 2005.
21. Needleman, *Money and the Meaning of Life*, p. 87.

The liberalism of the Enlightenment threw off traditional restraints on private economic initiative. Notions of an economy designed to serve just ends no longer dominated Western thought; the church's teachings, including prohibitions of usury, were deemed less relevant in a world where the pursuit of self-interest — including self-enrichment — was encouraged as a social good. These radical changes ushered in the Industrial Revolution and the modern period. Even today, Enlightenment assumptions undergird the popular notion that each individual is responsible for seeking his or her own happiness and prosperity, restrained only by the need to avoid infringing on the ability of others to do likewise.

We must not lose sight of how starkly these norms contrast with older biblical and theological teachings that counsel against the pursuit of personal riches and maintain that God requires selflessness and sacrificial generosity.

On Sunday mornings in contemporary America, Christians are subjected to mixed messages that generally accommodate our consumption-oriented culture. Robert Wuthnow finds evidence of this in a landmark study revealing that weekly churchgoers are deeply conflicted about the relationship between faith and money. More than half said that they had recently thought about what the Bible teaches on the subject, and more than eight in ten agreed that "being greedy is a sin against God," but just 16 percent said they were ever taught that it is wrong to "want a lot of money." Whether or not such desires automatically equate to greed, many had difficulty defining just what greed is. When asked to use a ten-point scale to indicate how much they admired certain types of people, 77 percent of weekly churchgoers gave a rating of eight or higher to "people who make a lot of money by working hard," while only 64 percent gave a rating this high to "people who work hard but never make much money."[22]

To be sure, today's church comprises a broad spectrum of theological and economic diversity, so generalizations do not

22. Robert Wuthnow, *God and Mammon in America* (New York: Free Press, 1994), pp. 121-31.

easily apply. But insofar as Wuthnow's findings are indicative of church teachings (or a lack thereof) on money, we may well conclude that American believers are led to deem the pursuit of wealth more admirable than sinful. Although some sects and monastic orders adhere to doctrines calling for simple living and renunciation of wealth, they account for a small minority of the nation's Christians. They also are less vocal.

The rise of megachurches (those with more than 2,000 members) in recent decades has been accompanied by jaw-dropping examples of personal and institutional extravagance — from luxurious facilities costing tens of millions of dollars to clergy paychecks rivaling those of corporate executives. This group often includes proponents of so-called prosperity theology, like the aptly named Creflo A. Dollar, a well-known pastor whose World Changers Church International in Georgia bankrolled his purchases of two Rolls Royce automobiles and regular travel on a private Gulfstream 3 jet aircraft. "I practice what I preach," he told *BusinessWeek* magazine, "and the Bible says . . . that God takes pleasure in the prosperity of his servants."[23] A respondent to Wuthnow's survey had similarly reconciled faith and the drive to be wealthy, explaining that her beautiful home, stylish clothes, and expensive travel are signs of divine blessing. "I know that God has given me all these things. So I'm not going to fret about getting more and more and more."[24]

Even churches that do not adhere to such doctrines are often quite unabashed about celebrating wealth. *Christianity Today* ran a cover story on evangelical churches entitled "We're in the Money!" that observed, "It is a bit surprising that we have displayed so little ambivalence at the wealth that is now in our hands."[25]

23. William Symonds et al., "Earthly Empires: How Evangelical Churches Are Borrowing from the Business Playbook," *BusinessWeek*, 23 May 2005, accessed online at http://www.businessweek.com/magazine/content/05_21/b3934001_mz001.htm.

24. Wuthnow, *God and Mammon in America*, p. 137.

25. Michael S. Hamilton, "We're in the Money!" *Christianity Today*, 12 June 2001, p. 42.

So it is that some churches embrace money-talk with gusto, while others tiptoe around the subject except when necessary to raise the annual church budget. In either case, little serious attention is given to the practical concerns of working people struggling to apply their faith to questions of money in their own lives.

More often, major church bodies have taken the easier route of critiquing the macro-economic system and its injustices.[26] They issue studies and pronouncements on economic policy, the moral shortcomings of capitalism, the effects of globalization, and other important matters that are not easily connected by Christians to their daily lives. Almost never do these pronouncements offer much help for living and working within an imperfect and frequently unjust system. Too often, these macro-economic statements suggest to individuals that the church is hostile not only to the system but also to the people who participate in it by going to work. Where the pre-Reformation church concerned itself with the economic life of the individual but had little to say about economic systems, the opposite is largely the case today.

One thing that has not changed over the centuries is the degree to which the culture's prevailing views of money tend to seep into the church's own thinking. Writing in *The Christian Century*, Lillian Daniel contends, "It is in its attitude toward money that the church is most likely to conform to the ways of the world rather than to transcend them." She adds, "Wrestling with money theologically is a mark of excellent ministry."[27]

26. Examples include *Vocation and Work* (Louisville: Committee on Social Witness Policy, Presbyterian Church USA, 1990); *Caritas in Veritate*, Encyclical Letter of Pope Benedict XVI (Vatican: Roman Catholic Church, 2009); *Centesimus annus*, Encyclical Letter of Pope John Paul II (Vatican: Roman Catholic Church, 1991); *Economic Justice for All*, Pastoral Letter of the National Conference of Catholic Bishops (Washington, D.C.: U.S. Catholic Conference, 1986); *Christian Faith and Economic Life* (New York: United Church Board for World Ministries, United Church of Christ, 1987); and "The Oxford Declaration on Christian Faith and Economics," *Transformation* 7, no. 2 (April-June 1990): 7-18.

27. Lillian Daniel, "Can We Talk? About Money? Affluent Christians," *The Christian Century*, 8 February 2003, p. 26.

Few pastors would claim this distinction for their own ministries. Even the most experienced may confess that they are not adept at thinking theologically about the role of money in the church, and that this makes it all the more difficult to speak confidently about the subject with their congregations.

The problem of money has troubled Christians since the earliest times. The church has never quite found a consensus on how to reconcile the biblical injunctions to give thanks to God for wealth and also to renounce any desire for it. This ambivalence widens the chasm between the worlds of faith and work, for the subject of work cannot be fully addressed apart from the making and spending of money. Before exploring strategies for closing this gap, we will consider how it is possible for many Christians to cope by compartmentalizing their lives, dividing themselves between the two worlds of faith and work.

Questions to Consider

- To pray for "neither poverty nor riches" is difficult to imagine in today's culture. Do you think Christians should ask God *not* to make them wealthy?
- Is it possible to reconcile biblical teachings on wealth with today's business mantra to maximize profits?
- Lillian Daniel believes few churches are willing to "wrestle with money theologically." Why do you think this is so?

CHAPTER FOUR

Divided Worlds, Divided Lives

In *The Big Kahuna,* a 1999 film starring Danny DeVito, Kevin Spacey, and Woody Harrelson, three salesmen go to a convention in hopes of meeting an elusive prospective customer whose contract could be the answer to their company's slumping sales of industrial lubricants. When the youngest of the group mentions that he spoke with the man at a party, the others are thrilled; but their mood quickly dims when he admits he took the opportunity to share his Christian faith and never got around to talking business. One of them quips acidly, "Did you happen to talk about what brand of lubricant Jesus would use?"

Later, when the two older men are alone, one asks the other, "Haven't you just wondered about God — ever?" His friend attempts to brush the question aside, but he persists. "I don't know why, but I've always had the haunting feeling that I had some kind of mission here on earth." Without hesitating, the other assures him that he does indeed have a mission: to be a salesman.

Just what does it mean to *be* a salesman — or an accountant or a police officer, for that matter? In our society, identification with occupational roles is a powerful force in defining who we are, for better or for worse. "This is Susan. She's a teacher." "Carlos is an auto mechanic." These roles influence how we think, speak, and act, and often give us a place of belonging among others with common interests. Role identification is so strong, in fact, that counselors say the loss of a job can be a devastating loss of identity.

Work roles also help shape our engagement with the world around us. We may come to accept, for example, that a salesperson should discuss lubricants but not religion. In some respects, this is inevitable and even necessary. But as roles define what counts as important, we may find it harder to attend fully to the larger human and spiritual dimensions of our activities.

Surely we do not consciously choose this, so how does it happen? The ethicist William May ascribes some blame to educators for this narrowing of identity, especially in the highly specialized professions. "As the institution that trains the modern professional, the university has done a brilliant job of equipping the professional with technical competence, but it has not always accepted responsibility for nourishing that moral substance and cultivating those virtues which a society has a right to expect in professionals."[1] No doubt educational institutions bear substantial responsibility for constricting the moral parameters of a host of occupations. But as we have discussed, historical and social factors, including workplace culture and even church teachings, tend to set the workplace apart as a sphere where moral and spiritual values important in other areas of life may not apply.

Peter Baelz worries that the postmodern world has largely abandoned the possibility of broadly shared values that can underlie and unite all areas of life:

So it is that in most Western industrialized countries church and society have lost their identity, religion has become more and more a private affair, and morality has become secular. This process affects both the structure of society and the consciousness of individuals. Institutions become independent of each other and establish their own rules and regulations. Individuals interpret life in non-religious ways. Religious beliefs lose their plausibility and no longer serve to provide a single co-

---

1. William F. May, *The Physician's Covenant* (Philadelphia: Westminster Press, 1983), p. 196.

hesive moral pattern. Instead, individuals and groups fashion their own ideals and society is held together by a minimal morality which is sufficient to make life in society possible.[2]

A new moral relativism has emerged where standards and values vary by context, organization, and role. If our salesman follows the advice of Albert Carr, discussed earlier, he may learn to see himself as a game player who is morally justified in using deception to persuade a customer to make a purchase, yet who remains scrupulously honest in his role as a parent. In quiet moments he may allow himself to ponder this inconsistency and even wonder which role is closer to his true identity. He suspects that a sufficient answer to the question "Who am I?" requires more than his name, his job title, or even a DNA sample. He is drawn to bigger questions: What is good and worthy of my devotion? What does this have to do with selling industrial lubricants? What are God's intentions for this world, and how can my work fit into this plan? For the postmodern Christian, unlike the believer of Luther's time, these questions demand not just universal answers, but individual ones. The salesman not only wonders what it means to lead a good life; he must know what this means *for him* in his particular situation.[3]

All of us can sympathize with the salesman's desire to discover God's mission for his life, but are unsurprised when he is discouraged by his friend, who would rather avoid such questions altogether. In our interviews with church members, we saw that many who acknowledged the faith-work divide had simply

2. Peter Baelz, *Ethics and Belief* (New York: Seabury Press, 1977), p. 66.

3. The philosopher Charles Taylor writes, "What does answer this question for us is an understanding of what is of crucial importance to us. To know who I am is a species of knowing where I stand. My identity is defined by the commitments and identifications which provide the frame or horizon within which I can try to determine from case to case what is good, or valuable, or what ought to be done, or what to endorse or oppose. In other words, it is the horizon within which I am capable of taking a stand." See Charles Taylor, *Sources of the Self: The Making of Modern Identity* (Cambridge, Mass.: Harvard University Press, 1989), p. 27.

learned to live with it. A technology manager at a large public company admitted, "I don't know why my life is so compartmentalized, but it feels comfortable that way."

How We Divide Our Lives

How is it that many sincere Christians seem so comfortable relegating their faith to the inner or private sphere, far from work? The explanation must lie in our human capacity to move with ease from one social role to another, conforming to the expectations that come with each, yet seldom allowing ourselves to confront the inconsistencies this creates in our lives. This is a form of self-deception that has been analyzed by theologians, philosophers, psychologists, sociologists, anthropologists, and even legal and political theorists.

Where the self of modernity was vaunted as a locus of rationality, autonomy, and individual freedom, the de-centered and splintered self of postmodernity is described by Anthony C. Thiselton as no longer "regarding itself as an active agent carving out any possibility with the aid of natural and social sciences, but as an opaque product of variable roles and performances which have been imposed upon it by the constraints of society and by its own inner drives and conflicts."[4]

All of this amounts to a loss of authenticity. Among those concerned about this phenomenon are philosophers like the existentialist Jean-Paul Sartre, who describes it as "bad faith" with oneself. He uses the examples of a waiter, a grocer, a tailor, and an auctioneer to illustrate how people in employment situations gradually become "nothing more" than the roles they play, "beings for others," to use Sartre's term, who merely act out their parts in the ways that are expected. "A grocer who dreams is offensive to the buyer, because such a grocer is not wholly a grocer.

4. Anthony C. Thiselton, *Interpreting God and the Postmodern Self: On Meaning, Manipulation, and Promise* (Grand Rapids: Wm. B. Eerdmans, 1995), p. 121.

Society demands that he limit himself to his function as a grocer . . . ," just as our salesman's friend insists he need be *nothing more* than a salesman.[5] Highly skilled professionals may be even more likely to collapse personal identity into their work roles.

Another helpful account is rendered by the contemporary philosopher Alasdair MacIntyre, who uses the term "characters" to describe roles endemic to particular contexts. Certain roles "furnish recognizable characters and the ability to recognize them is socially crucial because a knowledge of the character provides an interpretation of the actions of those individuals who have assumed the character." It follows, therefore, that roles and moral obligations are linked, leading to an *is* premise that entails an *ought* conclusion.[6] A woman is a lawyer; therefore, she ought to be and do whatever it is that a lawyer ought to be and do. MacIntyre is careful to contrast his concept with Sartre's, for he does not agree that the self becomes identical with, or "nothing but," a given role. Rather, he sees social roles as masks that we put on or take off as we move from one context to another.[7] The corporate manager's mask, he says, allows him or her to focus solely on maximizing efficiency when at work, making it easier to treat people as means rather than as ends.[8]

MacIntyre further shows that self-identification with a role can lead to "a separation of spheres of existence, a moral distancing of each social role from each of the others."[9] He rightly points to work roles as often the most dominant in our lives, influencing or even superseding the other roles with which we

5. Jean-Paul Sartre, *Being and Nothingness*, trans. Hazel E. Barnes (New York: Philosophy Library, Inc., 1956), pp. 221, 59.

6. Alasdair MacIntyre, *After Virtue* (Notre Dame: University of Notre Dame Press, 1981), p. 54.

7. MacIntyre, *After Virtue*, p. 28.

8. MacIntyre, *After Virtue*, p. 34. For a challenge to MacIntyre's view of the manager, see Kathryn Balstad Brewer, "Management as a Practice: A Response to Alasdair MacIntyre," *Journal of Business Ethics* 16, no. 8 (1 June 1997): 825-33.

9. Alasdair MacIntyre, "Corporate Modernity and Moral Judgment: Are They Mutually Exclusive?" in *Ethics and Problems of the Twenty-First Century*, ed. Kenneth Goodpaster and K. M. Sayre (Notre Dame: University of Notre Dame Press, 1979), pp. 122, 126.

strongly identify. Striving at work to gain the acceptance and approval of others, we often compete vigorously for opportunities and rewards. It would be a mistake to underestimate the psychological effect of finding one's place in a group that endeavors daily to gain the rewards of shared success.

It is undeniable, of course, that some of the social norms which apply at work may not, and should not, apply in other contexts. But to accept that *morality* may vary by role requires Christians to deny the truth that all persons and groups must finally be assessed in light of God's consistent purposes for all of creation.[10]

In psychology, too, some researchers tell us that mentally healthy people may comprise multiple selves, or "interacting subsystems," based on roles adapted to the habits, skills, attitudes, and values appropriate to their contexts.[11] Each social setting (e.g., work, church, family) stimulates the emergence of the most suitable self. One study cites "the person who easily distinguishes between his personal life and his professional life and who comfortably acts in routine conformity with each setting despite the fact that the conventional standards of the two settings contradict each other. The untroubled action in either setting . . . might come under the rubric of self-deception, since we have here a person whose actions endorse one standard while 'covertly' endorsing another, contradictory standard."[12] In this way, a Christian's role at work may serve temporarily to unburden her of Christ's moral demands, even as she continues to observe these standards outside the workplace.

10. See Stanley Hauerwas, *A Community of Character* (Notre Dame: University of Notre Dame Press, 1981), p. 105: "Christians are forbidden to despair in the face of the dividedness of the world. On the contrary, we are commanded to witness to others that there is a God that overcomes our differences by making them serve his Kingdom. The task of the Christian is not to defeat relativism by argument but to witness to a God who requires confrontation."

11. Stephen L. White, "Self-Deception and Responsibility for the Self," in *Perspectives on Self-Deception*, ed. Brian P. McLaughlin and Amelie Oksenberg Rorty (Berkeley and Los Angeles: University of California Press, 1988), p. 452.

12. Benzion Chanowitz and Ellen J. Langer, "Self-Protection and Self-Inception," in *Self-Deception and Self-Understanding*, ed. Mike W. Martin (Lawrence, Kans.: University Press of Kansas, 1985), pp. 124-25.

A 1987 episode of the U.S. public television series *Ethics in America* demonstrated that a news reporter's identification with his role could supersede even a sense of moral responsibility for human life. In a panel discussion, a hypothetical question was posed to Peter Jennings, lead news anchor for a major television network in the United States: If he and his camera crew were traveling with a company of enemy troops when they unexpectedly spotted a small group of American soldiers approaching at a distance, would he simply "roll tape" and watch the impending ambush of the Americans? James Fallows recounts Jennings' response and the debate that ensued:

> Jennings sat silent for about fifteen seconds. . . . "Well, I guess I wouldn't," he finally said. "I am going to tell you now what I am feeling, rather than the hypothesis I drew for myself. . . . I think that I personally would do what I could to warn the Americans."
>
> "Even if that means losing the story?" [moderator Charles] Ogletree asked.
>
> "Even though it would almost certainly mean losing my life," Jennings replied. . . .
>
> "I am astonished, really," at Jennings's answer, [competing network reporter Mike] Wallace said a moment later. He turned to Jennings and began to lecture him: "You're a *reporter*. . . ."
>
> Ogletree pushed Wallace. Didn't Jennings have some higher duty, either patriotic or human, to do something rather than just roll film as the soldiers from his own country were being shot?
>
> "No," Wallace said flatly and immediately. "You don't have a higher duty. No. No. You're a reporter!"
>
> Jennings backtracked fast. Wallace was right, he said. "I chickened out."[13]

For Wallace, it seems, a reporter on the job must be *nothing more* than a reporter. His impassioned response to Jennings il-

13. James Fallows, *Breaking the News* (New York: Vintage Books, 1997), pp. 12-14.

lustrates how colleagues often act to keep each other in character. We thus see how the primacy of roles in a profession may lessen one's sense of personal accountability for moral consequences, so long as one's actions are condoned by the standards of the group or institution.

J. Irwin Miller, past chairman of Cummins Engine Company, observes that Christian executives often succeed in dividing their lives, learning to live comfortably with conflicting, role-based moralities:

> One can simply wall [faith commitments] off from the difficult demands of business life and the real world. Sir John Bowring, who was in 1854 Superintendent of British Trade in China, could precipitate and win the second opium war with China, and over fierce Chinese resistance, force the Chinese to introduce Indian opium into their country. During the same years this man of many talents could compose and leave for us the great hymns "God is love; His mercy brightens/All the path in which we rove," as well as "Watchman, tell us of the night,/What its signs of promise are," and "In the cross of Christ I glory,/Towering o'er the wrecks of time."[14]

It's no secret that a tendency to moral relativism also predominates in politics, where officials who think of themselves as virtuous people may espouse personal values bearing little resemblance to their own actions or expected political behavior. Reinhold Niebuhr illustrates this by recalling a remark by Frederick the Great: "I hope that posterity will distinguish the philosopher from the monarch in me and the decent man from the politician. I must admit that when drawn into the vortex of European politics it is difficult to preserve decency and integrity. . . ."[15]

14. J. Irwin Miller, "How Religious Commitments Shape Corporate Decisions," *Harvard Divinity Bulletin,* February-March 1984, p. 5.
15. Reinhold Niebuhr, *The Nature and Destiny of Man,* vol. 1 (New York: Charles Scribner's Sons, 1941), p. 209.

When our roles as employees, church members, parents, or citizens conflict with each other — something sociologists call "role strain" — we sometimes find ourselves bargaining with ourselves. The philosopher Immanuel Kant conjectures that human beings possess a "twofold" nature or "doubled self," one portion of which is an "inner judge whom we conceive as another person."[16] To avoid self-condemnation and to lessen role strain, we may allow ourselves to accept that what counts as moral or immoral, as important or unimportant, is relative to the situation or role in which the distinction is made.

The irony of this should not be lost on Christians. The more we wish to think of ourselves as faithful and moral people, the more prone we may be to rely on self-deception to maintain this preferred belief in the face of our own shortcomings. We may amplify anything that confirms a desired view of ourselves while giving little weight to evidence that we are falling short. St. Augustine recognizes this spiritually perilous tendency to overestimate ourselves when he confesses, "My sin was all the more incurable because I thought I was not a sinner."[17]

Theologian Stanley Hauerwas points to former Nazi leader Albert Speer, whom the BBC called "the Nazi who said 'Sorry,'" as one whose identity was almost completely subsumed by his role as a government bureaucrat and architect.[18] Hauerwas believes that Speer's identification with his official role made it possible for him to avoid confronting the inconsistencies in his life. Roles provide "a ready vehicle for self-deception, since we

16. Immanuel Kant, *The Doctrine of Virtue,* trans. Mary J. Gregor (Philadelphia: University of Pennsylvania Press, 1964), p. 94.

17. St. Augustine, *The Confessions,* trans. F. J. Sheed (New York: Sheed & Ward, 1942), p. 28.

18. Stanley Hauerwas, *Truthfulness and Tragedy* (Notre Dame: University of Notre Dame Press, 1977), p. 94. See also Hauerwas, *A Community of Character,* pp. 101-8: "The source of each tragedy is a situation in which a character's multiple responsibilities and obligations conflict not only with self-interest, but with each other. Moral choice is potentially tragic when several moral obligations are juxtaposed with the necessity of a single decision having irreversible consequences."

can easily identify with them without any need to spell out what we are doing," he writes.[19]

Even the church has been guilty of unwittingly encouraging role-based compartmentalization. A misreading of Luther's doctrine of the "two kingdoms" has led to the view "that the Christian — who must also participate in the temporal kingdom as a father or mother, a citizen or soldier — [should surrender] the identifying marks of his Christianity the moment he enters the worldly sphere," writes Helmut Thielicke, a Lutheran. The result is "two spheres of existence which have nothing to do with one another, spheres which are subject to very different laws and which divide the Christian person — through whom the dividing frontier passes — into two completely separate and isolated segments."[20]

Thielicke worries that this misunderstanding of Luther leads easily to a moral dualism, where the "inner person" acts within the kingdom of God in pursuit of divine goodness, while the "outer person" adheres to the moral standards of a world where power and self-seeking are ultimate. Luther may have foreseen this danger, for he attempted to build in safeguards against a double morality or the establishment of "a sphere where Christ's teachings do not apply."[21] In fact, he taught that love of neighbor is the overriding commandment governing all spheres, making every job an opportunity to do God's business.

By contrast, the Reformed theology of John Calvin is less prone to distinguish between two kingdoms, for God's law is seen as a present Word with normative significance not only in the faith community but also in public life. "The relation between Christ and the world is fully as direct as the relation between Christ and the church. In both relations what is at stake is the one universal lordship."[22] Although Calvin's theology may be

---

19. Hauerwas, *Truthfulness and Tragedy*, p. 87.

20. Helmut Thielicke, *Theological Ethics*, vol. 1, ed. William H. Lazareth (Philadelphia: Fortress Press, 1966), pp. 362-63.

21. Thielicke, *Theological Ethics*, vol. 1, pp. 377-78.

22. Helmut Thielicke, *Theological Ethics*, vol. 2, ed. William H. Lazareth (Philadelphia: Fortress Press, 1969), p. 592.

less inclined to rationalize relativism, we have seen that Christians today are nonetheless influenced by the church's implicit categorization of human activities as secular or sacred, temporal or eternal, public or private.

Cultural and Institutional Pressures

The church's public influence is waning as Western society undergoes a gradual shift that leaves Christians less certain of how — or whether — their faith should inform their priorities and purposes at work or in other arenas of public life. Today's believer might reasonably ask by what authority a theologically conceived morality proposes to guide or judge individual action within non-religious institutions. Is it sensible or even fair to insist that the will of God revealed in Scripture should be given equal weight by Christians in all human activities, roles, or contexts?

This question does not lend itself to neat or uncomplicated answers, which is why Jacques Ellul believes we are tempted to "dissociate the spiritual situation from the material one, despising the material situation, denying that it has any meaning, declaring that it is neutral and does not concern eternal life. . . ."[23] We learn to subvert self-awareness to avoid the difficulty of reconciling the high aspirations of faith and the harsh realities of work. We no longer give our full attention to the activities of which we are a part or even to the harm resulting from our actions or inaction.

Workplace culture frequently supports this division of consciousness. As individuals we may find that the values derived from faith are not always reflected in the collective behaviors of the groups with which we identify at work. This is not to suggest that organizations are incapable of acting morally, nor is it to minimize the potential of one person's moral agency to affect the work environment. But the fact remains that organizations gen-

23. Jacques Ellul, *The Presence of the Kingdom* (Colorado Springs: Helmers & Howard, 1989), p. 7.

erally have greater influence on individuals than *vice versa*.[24] Robert Solomon reminds us that the workplace "defines not only jobs and roles and rules for proper behavior; it also sets goals and establishes what counts as success. It circumscribes one's probable circle of friends, both directly, by setting up peer relationships and arranging daily face-to-face introductions, and indirectly, by cultivating characteristic ambitions, aspirations, and expectations. . . ."[25]

Individuals at work tend to adopt the habits and attitudes of the group without recognizing the subtle coercion and pressures that cause them to do so. This subordination of the will of the individual to the power of the group is at the root of much workplace stress. In the sociological analysis of Robert Jackall, this is the "enduring genius of the organizational form," wherein individuals may retain a diversity of private beliefs and motives as long as they keep them to themselves and conform to others' expectations on the job. "As a result, bureaucratic work causes people to bracket, while at work, the moralities that they might hold outside the workplace or that they might adhere to privately and to follow instead the prevailing morality of the particular organizational situation."[26]

Our sense of *who we are* is subtly formed by all of these factors and is reinforced daily by interacting with those who share our experiences and participate in a common story. As MacIntyre explains, "I can only answer the question 'What am I to do?'

24. Primary research among corporate managers finds that individuals perceive incongruity between their personal ethical commitments and the expectations of their employers. "In particular, many managers appear pressured to compromise their values to achieve organizational goals and to advance their careers. . . . The conflict between personal values and ethics and those demanded for success may have dysfunctional consequences for both individuals and organizations." See Peter E. Mudrack and E. Sharon Mason, "Individual Ethical Beliefs and Perceived Organizational Interests," *Journal of Business Ethics* 15 (1996): 851.

25. Robert C. Solomon, *The New World of Business: Ethics and Free Enterprise in the Global 1990s* (Lanham, Md.: Rowman & Littlefield, 1994), p. 139.

26. Robert Jackall, *Moral Mazes* (New York: Oxford University Press, 1988), p. 6.

if I can answer the question 'Of what story or stories do I find myself a part?'" In other words, personal identity is not formed in isolation, for "the story of my life is always embedded in the story of those communities from which I derive my identity."[27] The formation of identity involves seeing oneself within a unified structure of meaning, very often represented by one's work. For Christians, places of worship and places of employment offer identity-defining narratives that may at times be hard to reconcile with each other.

The Distortion of Legalism

Let us now return briefly to our discussion of the nature of business, which we began in Chapter One. We have seen that a tendency toward *legalism* is a common mode of thinking in business, governmental, and professional organizations, whereby questions of moral or human obligation are subjected solely to technical rules or laws. This is a form of moral relativism where individuals allow the law or company rules to define limited moral standards for work-related conduct — even as these same individuals continue to avow supra-legal obligations in other areas of life, such as home, church and neighborhood. Carr's poker analogy advocates just this way of thinking, urging businesspeople to take advantage of every legally permissible strategy to make as much money as possible, while assuring them that "openheartedness" is out of place, both in poker and in business.

James Fieser is another author who thinks moral responsibilities in business should be limited strictly to what the law specifies. He builds his case on three arguments:

1. A moral obligation is valid only if an agent can be reasonably expected to perform that obligation.
2. In our society, business people cannot be reasonably expected to perform obligations above what the law requires.

27. MacIntyre, *After Virtue*, pp. 201, 205.

3. Therefore, in our society, business people do not have moral obligations above what the law requires.[28]

"Our society lacks a homogenous source of external morality . . . ," he argues. "The moral mandates which remain (external to the legal system) do not have the backing of society to carry universal prescriptive force."[29] He concludes that extra-legal obligations "appear to be optional; and it is unreasonable to expect business people to be obligated to principles which appear to be optional."[30] While he does not rule out the possibility of an "ideal standard of morality," he insists that all of society's agreed-upon moral expectations of business and businesspeople are already expressed in the law.

Contrast this philosophy with the actions taken by Bob, the CEO who urged his management team to be guided by love in dealing with employees facing layoffs. For him, the ideal standard was the teaching of Jesus Christ, raising the bar considerably higher than the requirements of civil law. Apparently Bob did not think this was unreasonable.

Jacques Ellul stresses that Christ's example is "neither that of an absolutizing nor of a spiritualizing of the law, [for] there was never any question of doing less than the law required. It was a matter of going infinitely farther."[31] We succumb to legalistic thinking when we fail to do what we know is best simply because no rule requires us to do it, or when we feel free to do as we please simply because no rule explicitly prohibits it. Circum-

---

28. James Fieser, "Do Businesses Have Moral Obligations Beyond What the Law Requires?" *Journal of Business Ethics* 15 (1996): 462. Fieser cites what he believes are shortcomings of Carr's and Milton Friedman's well-known arguments, rejecting the view that business has any additional moral obligations on the grounds that such obligations impose "unreasonable expectations."

29. Fieser, "Do Businesses Have Moral Obligations Beyond What the Law Requires?" p. 462.

30. Fieser, "Do Businesses Have Moral Obligations Beyond What the Law Requires?" p. 463.

31. Jacques Ellul, *To Will and to Do* (Philadelphia: Pilgrim Press, 1969), p. 254.

stances where moral obligation cannot be reduced to fixed, determinate rules are not the rare exception but are the most common part of our daily interactions. A legalistic view of rules, detached from the relationships they are meant to govern, actually violates the spirit of the law and distorts our relationships with others, including God.

I regularly ask undergraduate business students to recall an ethical issue they personally have encountered in their public lives, either at work or in another organization. The class then divides into small groups to share experiences and choose an issue for a more careful analysis. A recent example was the experience of a student who had worked as a trucking company's bill collector, telephoning past-due customers to demand payment. During one call he learned that the delinquent customer was seriously ill and unable to pay on time. Should he turn the account over to a collection agency, as was company policy, or should he speak with his boss about making an exception to allow the customer more time? His classmates in the small group did not see an ethical dilemma, insisting "a contract is a contract" — no exceptions, no questions asked. "We want to be hard-nosed businesspeople," they proclaimed. The legal obligations of the contract were all that mattered to them. Others in the class countered that the situation called for compassion and finding a way to extend the terms of payment.

Again, our interest here is not the law *per se,* but the error of allowing the demands of the law to define the extent of human obligations. Few Christians who accept this way of thinking at work would be comfortable with such a constricted morality on a personal level. What if the standard of behavior in our homes were defined solely by the law, making anything permissible so long as it is legal?

In these four chapters we have explored the gap separating faith and work. Business culture does its part to divide these spheres of life, but the church is also culpable for devaluing the daily work of Christians in "secular" vocations. The roots of this failure run deep in the church's own traditions and doctrines, including its centuries-old struggle to come to terms with money — and the desire for wealth — in the Christian life. Faced with these divisive influences, many believers learn to compartmentalize their lives, resigned to take faith more seriously in private life than in public life. The philosopher Jacob Needleman warns that "it will do us no good merely to pursue strong expectations of the inner world unless we are pointed toward equally strong experiences that will enable us to contact both worlds simultaneously. That is, we need to find an awareness that can be in contact with the two worlds."[32]

In the next section, we will consider a theological framework that may help us think about these problems and bring greater coherence to our lives. Such a theology must be relevant to the realities of business and professional life, yet able to challenge the assumptions that have long rendered the church ineffective in equipping people for faithful living in the workplace. We will find no easy answers or quick fixes, but perhaps it is possible to clarify what it means to be a disciple in the world of work.

Questions to Consider

- Some argue that the only ethical obligations of business-people are those defined by the law. Do you agree that it is unrealistic to expect Christians in the workplace to assume ethical responsibilities that go beyond what the law requires?
- How have your roles and experiences at work helped shape your sense of personal identity?
- Do you ever feel that your identity at work must differ from who you are at home or church? If so, has this made it more difficult for you to live out a consistent faith in all areas of your life?

---

32. Jacob Needleman, *Money and the Meaning of Life* (New York: Doubleday, 1991), p. 167.

PART II

TOWARD COHERENCE

CHAPTER FIVE

Rethinking Christian Vocation

"God called me out of AT&T," the man said as we finished lunch. He had left his corporate position to join a for-profit enterprise founded with a mission to serve the poor in Eastern Europe, Africa, and other developing regions. The company was creating jobs and economic development by starting profitable micro-enterprises that also help fund local ministries. (We will return to the concept of "business as mission" in Chapter Seven.)

I was impressed by the company's track record, but those few words stuck with me for several days afterwards. *"God called me out of AT&T."* It had a familiar ring, similar to so many other testimonies from people who have left careers to join the clergy or work in a mission field. It is easy to see how one may sense a divine calling to such work, but are we as willing to accept that it may actually be God's intention for someone to *remain* at AT&T or Wal-Mart — or the Internal Revenue Service, for that matter? In discussing the church's implicit hierarchy of occupations (in Chapter Two), we noted that Christians are seldom encouraged to think of "secular" work as truly important to God.

At this point in our study we must inquire into the purpose and meaning of work in the Christian life. Theologians have seldom treated work as a central category or organizing concept; however, some encouraging recent efforts are reclaiming older theological insights to re-conceptualize what may be called a "doctrine of vocation."[1]

Drawing on the Reformers' ideas, they remind us that while work may benefit the individual worker, God places greater value on its contribution to human sustenance. The Scriptures affirm even the most basic forms of work, not necessarily because they yield individual wealth or even happiness, but because they nourish life and prevent suffering (e.g., Gen. 3:19; Prov. 14:23; Prov. 20:13; Eccles. 9:10; 2 Thess. 3:10-11).

John Calvin invoked these teachings when he insisted that all must work — rich and poor alike. He saw this not only as God's will, but as a means of demonstrating that one is among the elect. The notion that idleness is a sign of being among the damned may strike twenty-first-century ears as questionable soteriology. Fortunately, however, Calvin and other Reformers bequeathed us a far more helpful insight — namely, that work is not merely a means of survival but is a service to God in the ongoing process of creating and ordering the world. In a similar vein, Martin Luther, a former monk who criticized the monastic life for its neglect of duty to neighbor, argued that all socially useful occupations are equally important in God's overall plan. A garbage collector, then, may be as necessary to the common good as a king or a teacher.

The Lost Meaning of Vocation

This is a helpful corrective, but a proper understanding of Christian *vocation* entails much more than this. Etymologically, the

---

1. Examples include Miroslav Volf, *Work in the Spirit: Toward a Theology of Work* (Eugene, Ore.: Wipf & Stock, 1991); Darrell Cosden, *A Theology of Work: Work and the New Creation* (Eugene, Ore.: Wipf & Stock, 2004); Armand Larive, *After Sunday: A Theology of Work* (New York: Continuum International Publishing, 2004); David A. Krueger, *Keeping Faith at Work* (Nashville: Abingdon Press, 1994); R. Paul Stevens, *The Other Six Days: Vocation, Work, and Ministry in Biblical Perspective* (Grand Rapids: Wm. B. Eerdmans, 1999).

word is derived from the Latin *vocare*, which literally means "to call." God calls each of us into the divine relationship, and we respond to this call through the living of our lives, including our lives at work. In today's usage, *vocation* has lost much of this richer meaning and is virtually synonymous with words like *occupation* and *career*. Vocational schools are places in our communities where people learn trades like plumbing and cosmetology.

William May notes that earlier Christians understood their primary calling as serving "not the private musings of the religiously adept but the flourishing of the community":

> The late sixteenth-century theologian William Perkins, who powerfully influenced the American Puritans, explicitly defined a calling as "a certain kind of life, ordained and imposed on man by God for the common good." In the language of the philosophers, God is the efficient cause of one's vocation — God does the calling; and the common good defines the final cause toward which the vocation points. Perkins did not tack on a reference to the common good casually.[2]

Perkins also condemned work in pursuit of wealth, worldly goods, or personal recognition, and spoke in the strongest terms against occupations that do not serve the good of all. "The modern choice of a career," May writes, "often depends precisely upon these honors, pleasures, profits, and worldly commodities," distracting us from obligations to others, including our families.[3] Over time, Puritanism evolved away from Perkins's principles and toward a more individualistic understanding of vocation that echoes Calvin's idea of work as a demonstration of personal salvation. We can see how this led the Puritans perilously close to "works righteousness," where salva-

---

2. William May, *Beleaguered Rulers: The Public Obligation of the Professional* (Louisville: Westminster John Knox Press, 2001), p. 15; the quotation is from William Perkins, "A Treatise of the Vocations or Callings of Men with Sorts and Kinds of Them, and the Right Use Thereof," in *Puritan Political Ideas*, ed. Edmund S. Morgan (Indianapolis: Bobbs-Merrill, 1963), p. 36.

3. May, *Beleaguered Rulers*, p. 16.

tion is earned by human actions rather than given by God as an unmerited gift of grace. Conversely, we can see how a belief that salvation *cannot* be earned causes many people to dismiss the value of temporal work as irrelevant to one's eternal relationship with God.

It was the Puritans as well who formulated a sometimes helpful distinction between a *primary* calling to follow Christ — the shared calling of all believers — and a *secondary* calling to do so in a particular context. Accordingly, every believer's identity and wholeness is in Christ, even as all who share this vocation are called to serve in many diverse ways. It is true that all believers share a primary call to discipleship, but we should be very cautious about classifying specific jobs as secondary callings, as this can lead to either pride or despair. Those fortunate enough to enjoy meaningful work may infer that they are somehow preferred by God over others. Those whose jobs feel like empty drudgery may despair that God has less regard for them.

Some contemporary theologies of vocation helpfully emphasize work as an integral part of the larger Christian life. In many of these accounts, work is seen as a response to God's initial intention for humankind to be stewards of the earth — tilling the soil, developing natural resources, ordering creation, and bettering the lives of others. Some go so far as to advance a more eschatological view of work, stressing a human role in moving this world toward the new creation to be ushered in ultimately by Christ's return.[4] There may be some truth in this, but as Ellul says, "God never proposes that people collectively should turn society into an earthly paradise," only that we should "fulfill his purposes in this environment and not some other."[5] We are to be as faithful as possible within the confines and limitations of our own situations, whatever and whenever they may be.

When today's church speaks of individuals being called to

4. See Volf, *Work in the Spirit*.

5. Jacques Ellul, *Money and Power* (Downers Grove, Ill.: InterVarsity Press, 1984), p. 27.

specific roles, especially in full-time Christian work, it too often implies that discerning God's call is primarily about matching ourselves with an occupation or a job already chosen for us by God. "God has a plan for your life," we may be told, with the implication that it is our task to unravel the mystery, just as the lubricant salesman attempted to do in the film *The Big Kahuna* (discussed in the previous chapter).

Certainly we should seek God's guidance when considering career choices, but Christians would do well to give much more attention to discerning God's will in their *current* situations. Are our lives the sum of random experiences, or has God's hand and providence brought us to a place where we may serve here and now?

Luther believed that Christians are called to service wherever they may be. However, he carried this idea too far by teaching that Christians should never seek to change jobs (despite having done so himself), a distortion of Paul's meaning in the admonition "each one should retain the place in life that the Lord assigned to him and to which God has called him" (1 Cor. 7:17). Misunderstanding this text, many Christians have concluded that there is one — and only one — divinely assigned occupation for each person, and that their life's goal is to find it. I personally know some believers for whom this misunderstanding has fueled unfulfilled hopes, anxiety, and even despair.

In the context of the rest of the letter to the church at Corinth, it is clear that Paul is counseling Christian converts not to make changes in their social or marital status *as a result of* their newfound faith. Even slaves are told not to be preoccupied with their status, though they are advised to take their freedom if it is offered.

Paul's larger message is that all belong to Christ, whatever their station in life, and that they should allow themselves to be used by God in the places where they live and work. Certainly he did not intend to make Christianity the defender of the *status quo* or to suggest that God has but one use for each person's gifts.

Moral Ambiguity: Is All Work God's Work?

The recent revival of interest in Christian vocation has been of much benefit to individuals and the church, but it has left unresolved some of the more difficult theological questions about work. Although Luther taught that all occupations serving useful purposes are of equal importance to God, he continued to see the clergy's calling as more sacred than others. Calvin generally agreed that all occupations serving "the common good of human beings are lawful and holy."[6] In this spirit it is popular for some ministries to encourage all Christians to think of their jobs as divine appointments. This well-intended advice may inspire some, but it ignores the obvious fact that some jobs seem to be more compatible with God's will than others.

On what basis is work deemed *good* work? Dietrich Bonhoeffer describes the early church's discomfort with many occupations considered inappropriate for Christians: "The actor who had to play the part of pagan gods and heroes, the teacher who was forced to teach pagan mythologies in pagan schools, the gladiator who had to take human life for sport, the soldier who wielded the sword, the policeman and the judge [who enforced oppressive laws], all had to renounce their heathen professions if they wanted to be baptized."[7]

Reformation theologians condemned sinful pursuits like theft, prostitution, usury, and idleness. Luther broadly denounced any work that is "sinful in itself," but he had no difficulty saying that a Christian's vocation could include service as an executioner.[8] Believers of good conscience, then and now, do not always agree on the criteria for legitimate occupations where Christians may live out God's call to discipleship. Within the Ref-

6. John Calvin, *Treatises against the Anabaptists and the Libertines*, ed. and trans. Benjamin Wirt Farley (Grand Rapids: Baker Books, 1988), p. 81.

7. Dietrich Bonhoeffer, *The Cost of Discipleship* (New York: Touchstone, 1995), p. 266.

8. Martin Luther, *Church Postil: Gospels: Advent, Christmas, and Epiphany Sermons*, vol. 1, in *The Precious and Sacred Writings of Martin Luther*, vol. X, ed. John N. Lenker (Minneapolis: Lutherans in All Lands, 1905), pp. 248-49.

ormation movement, Anabaptists were less liberal about the types of work that could be compatible with Christian vocation. Military service, which was approved by Luther, was forbidden by the Anabaptists' Schleitheim Confession of the Swiss Brethren (which also disdained all forms of civil service). Contemporary Christians still debate whether or not certain occupations are appropriate for believers.

To illustrate this, one of my doctoral students, the pastor of a low-wealth congregation in a minority community, shared with our class a dilemma he was then facing in his own parish. A controversy erupted when a longtime member, who also happened to be the church's most generous financial donor, was nominated to be a deacon. Some members strongly objected on the grounds that he was the proprietor of a local liquor store. "Everyone is happy for the church to take his money," the pastor told us, "but they can't abide the thought of a deacon in the liquor business." He paused and added, "Never mind that most of them are his customers during the week."

What would Luther say about this man's occupation? Possibly very little, for his wife, Katie, was known throughout the community for the beer and wine she made in their home. How would members of a wealthy Napa Valley congregation respond if the owner of a successful wine estate were nominated as a church officer?

Our class of pastors from nine diverse denominations had a lively discussion about the liquor store owner and whether his work could be squared with our understanding of Christian vocation. Some argued that his business served no social good and likely caused much misery in the community. Others countered that God needs Christians everywhere, maybe *especially* in a liquor store. "A lot of hurting people who come to his store would never enter a church," one pointed out. "Isn't it possible that God is using him in that place?" The class couldn't agree, but the case opened a broader conversation about what constitutes good work from a Christian perspective.

Other examples may be even more complex. Most of us would consider a "Christian pornographer" a preposterous oxymoron, but would we object to a Christian holding an executive post at a company like Time Warner that profits from pornographic content distributed via its cable system? What would we say about a Christian at an advertising agency who uses her creative talents to persuade people in developing countries to start smoking cigarettes? Or a Christian operating a chain of payday loan offices that capitalize on the misfortune of the poor?

Just as problematic are many jobs that serve others in legitimate ways, yet are destructive to the workers who perform them. Recall our earlier example of the woman earning minimum wage while standing eight hours a day to gut hundreds of chickens passing her on a hanging conveyor. Certainly God intends that some should work to feed others, but what if this work reduces a woman to an expendable part of an inhumane machine? Can this be *good* work in God's eyes? It is inevitable that many find it much harder to see God's purposes in their daily work than in their homes or churches or neighborhoods. How then should we view occupations that seem irreconcilable with God's desire for human flourishing? There are no easy answers.

Such questions may be best approached with an understanding of Christian vocation as an all-encompassing call to discipleship in every area of life. The theologian Karl Barth explains that the New Testament Greek word for vocation, *klesis,* refers not to specific occupations but "means quite unambiguously the divine calling, i.e., the act of the call of God issued in Jesus Christ by which a man is transplanted into his new state as a Christian." In Barth's understanding, vocation is a calling that transcends and integrates human spheres of activity and has "nothing to do with" God directing a person "to enter a special sphere of work."[9]

Clearly, some work is "sinful in itself" because of the harm it inflicts, but most jobs can be both life-giving and life-draining, providing opportunities to serve the good of others, while occa-

---

9. Karl Barth, *Church Dogmatics* III.4, *The Doctine of Creation,* ed. and trans. Geoffrey William Bromiley (London: T&T Clark International, 1961), p. 600.

sionally challenging us with great stress and ethical uncertainty. This is the real world inhabited by the Christians we interviewed — the manager who felt guilty about overworking and burning out her employees; the banker who administered a loan program he thought was designed to exploit low-income borrowers. There are times when one must ask if it is right to continue in work that seems antithetical to God's will, and the dilemma may be sharpened when options for alternative employment are few.

How, then, can a Christian know when to leave a job for moral or spiritual reasons? Sometimes the answer is obvious, as when some activity risks criminal liability. At other times it's a matter of gauging one's potential for changing things for the better. Can the loan administrator persuade his bank to change the policies that exploit the poor? Has he made a reasonable effort to do so? In prayerfully considering his options, he must try to discern whether God is leading him elsewhere, for leaving the situation will end any opportunity to influence the bank.

"Go in peace"

The Bible tells the story of a powerful man who comes to know God in a remarkable way, only to realize that the duties of his executive position are almost certainly an affront to God (2 Kings 5:1-19). Naaman is the commanding general of the army of Syria, a kingdom perpetually at war with Israel. He also suffers from leprosy, a frightful illness for which there is no cure.

In the unlikeliest of scenarios, a servant girl tells him of a prophet in Israel who may be able to cleanse him of the disease. Desperate enough to try anything, he asks his king for permission to travel to Israel for help. The Syrian monarch obliges and sends a letter to the king of Israel, asking him to receive Naaman and cure his leprosy. The Israelite king is stunned by the request and initially takes it for some kind of enemy trick. When he eventually sends Naaman and his royal entourage to seek help from Elisha, the prophet declines to meet the visitors but sends a messenger to tell Naaman to wash in the Jordan River seven times "and your flesh will be restored and you will be cleansed."

Naaman questions the idea that river water can cure anything, for he had expected the prophet to dramatically wave his hand over the leprosy in the fashion of a magician. But his friends convince him to go into the river, and he is completely cured. In one of Scripture's most dramatic moments of conversion, Naaman gives credit to the living God and exclaims, "Now I know that there is no God in all the world except in Israel." In fact, he is so sure that God lives only in one land that he takes two mule-loads of Israel's soil back to Syria to build a personal altar for worship.

Naaman realizes that when he returns home, his job will require him to kneel beside the king of Syria at the altar of the pagan idol Rimmon. He knows that this will be blasphemous and scandalous for a follower of the one true God. Even with his personal altar to Yahweh, he will appear to be participating in the worship of a false god. His public actions in the workplace will conflict with his personal faith.

Naaman is tormented by this inner conflict even before leaving Elisha's home. He does not ponder quitting his job or defecting to Israel's army, but instead seeks God's forgiveness for the sin he will commit when carrying out his duties. In a sense, his decision is consistent with Paul's later admonition to new converts to stay in their current situations.

Naaman shares his worries with Elisha in hopes that the prophet will mediate on his behalf for divine forgiveness. Elisha's response is as astonishing as it is simple: "Go in peace." Brimming with God's grace, these three words, says Jacques Ellul, are an "affirmation of the unity of Naaman's being":

> He [Elisha] offers no ethical advice. He does not tell him he ought to leave his post and background and refuse to bow down before idols. Elisha does not plunge into casuistry, differentiating what would be legitimate for him from what would not. He has no solution to propose. He lets Naaman choose himself. He lets him make his own decision. He faces him up to

his responsibility without saying what it is. Yet he does not let him go away empty. He grants him peace from God. He finally declares the gospel to him.[10]

"Go in peace." The prophet pronounces God's blessing with the assurance that it is possible for Naaman to be whole and undivided in his workplace. We know nothing of Naaman's life after this dramatic conversion, though subsequent texts reveal that the two nations remain at war, presumably with Naaman as the Syrian general in chief. Still, we must imagine that he rejoined the king's court for some good purpose. It is plausible that he went on to serve God in the Syrian palace, just as Joseph became premier of Egypt for a pharaoh, and Daniel rose to be a trusted adviser to Babylonian kings. Is it any less likely that God uses the service of today's believers in government offices, as well as in corporations, law firms, and factories?

To be sure, Christians should be unwilling to participate in some activities or even to hold certain jobs, but leaving a situation must always be weighed against the potential of staying for the benefit of others. Although either decision may be difficult, the latter usually takes an extra measure of courage and spiritual stamina.

While such stark choices are rare for most of us, workplace discipleship can be challenging even in the best of circumstances. Scripture is a source of metaphysical and moral truth, not an instruction manual for every situation that may arise at work. Each of us must respond to God's call in the unique context of our own circumstances. We cannot know the mind of God in all things; therefore, our vocation of discipleship is to become more like Christ, for *who we are* ultimately shapes what we do. God grants us freedom to explore and develop ourselves, and much of this activity occurs through work. This essential point is too often missing from church teachings on vocation.

Our next chapter will consider how a moral theology of work

10. Jacques Ellul, *The Politics of God and the Politics of Man* (Grand Rapids: Wm. B. Eerdmans, 1972), p. 39.

may help to shape authentic Christian discipleship in any arena of public life. Such a theology must be capable of critiquing cultural assumptions about vocation while providing an alternative framework based on God's revealed purposes. In the end it must be realistic and applicable to the broad scope of occupations held by Christians.

Questions to Consider

- The prophet Elisha tells Naaman to "go in peace," even though the Syrian general's job requires him to kneel publicly at a pagan altar. What might we learn from this?
- Can you think of some occupations that are simply incompatible with Christian discipleship? What criteria would you use to determine this?
- All Christians share a common vocation, regardless of where they work. How might this understanding of vocation help correct the church's hierarchical assumption that members of certain occupations have been singled out by God for more favored work?

CHAPTER SIX

A Moral Theology for Work

I was in the audience recently as a bank executive assured a group of three hundred college students that being a faithful Christian is the secret to business success. When he finished his remarks, someone asked him about the ethical challenges he had encountered on the job. Without hesitating, the executive replied glibly, "I have never found ethics to be a challenge. If you follow Jesus Christ in business, you will know the right thing to do, and you will do the right thing."

I was chagrined. This was less than helpful to a roomful of young people preparing for careers in professional fields where moral difficulties are more complex than ever. If anything, they needed to hear the sobering truth that followers of Jesus Christ may actually struggle with *more* ethical issues at work. Christian faith does not shield any of us from moral difficulty; it calls us to the hard work of being salt and light — of moral agency — in a world where God's justice and love are urgently needed.

If Christian wholeness is the alternative to a divided life, it often seems frustratingly elusive. Could it be that we, like this bank executive, mistake the Christian life for a smooth and gentle path? Albert Carr was not far from the truth in warning young people that taking their faith seriously at work might result in "an ulcer or a nervous tic." It is no wonder that many believers learn to avoid this stress by separating work life from faith life, seldom acknowledging to themselves the inconsistencies that arise as they move from one sphere or role to another.

We instinctively seek a more comfortable place to stand, either by capitulating to the ways of those around us or by withdrawing into a private faith. By contrast, authentic Christianity — with its goal of wholeness in all areas of life — requires us to actually *invite* discomfort by placing ourselves, in Jacques Ellul's words, "at the point of contact between two currents: the will of the Lord, and the will of the world."[1] For Christ's disciples are needed most in the very places where it is most difficult to stand.

What Is Required?

What, then, does it actually mean to be a disciple at work? A good starting point is found in the Old Testament book of Micah:

> "He has told you, O mortal, what is good;
> and what does the LORD require of you
> but to do justice, and to love kindness,
> and to walk humbly with your God?"
>
> (Mic. 6:8, NRSV)

Here is God's definition of good. Some translations substitute "mercy" for "kindness," but the effect is the same. These words are the culmination of a poetic drama where Israel is on trial and God is stating the case against the people. In the end, Israel has no defense, as the only righteous response to God's justice and kindness is for the people themselves to be just and kind — a reminder of the Levitical commandment "Be holy because I, the LORD your God, am holy" (Lev. 19:2). It is significant that the Hebrew word for "mortal" in this text refers to all of humankind and not to Israel alone.

1. Jacques Ellul, *The Presence of the Kingdom* (Colorado Springs: Helmers & Howard, 1989), p. 18.

These few lines sum up the two commandments Jesus named as the greatest — love God and love your neighbor. This is the heart of the Christian vocation of discipleship. "Everyone who loves has been born of God and knows God. Whoever does not love does not know God, because God is love" (1 John 4:7-8). We love others by acting justly and kindly because this is what God does for us. "And he has given us this command: Whoever loves God must also love his brother" (4:20). Christians are told to be "imitators of God" through "a life of love, just as Christ loved us and gave himself up for us . . ." (Eph. 5:1-2). If we wish to be like Christ, we must strive to love unconditionally and sacrificially.

The whole of Christian ethics rests on this simple but exceedingly demanding principle. What would it mean if we actually responded to God's redemptive grace by loving every person within our scope of influence at work? Are you capable of this? Am I? Fortunately, we are not on our own, says the nineteenth-century philosopher Søren Kierkegaard, for "when the eternal says, 'You shall love,' it becomes the eternal's responsibility to make sure it can be done."[2] Unconditional love is not within our power, but God makes it possible, provided we commit ourselves to developing this spiritual capacity.

An ethic of love goes beyond both duty (keeping promises, telling the truth, doing a job well) and compliance (with civil law, contractual requirements, or employment policies), both of which are necessary in the workplace. Love recognizes that every person is unique and must be cared for individually, whether or not a rule mandates it. This requires us to take the time and effort to discover what actually meets the other's needs.

It would be easy to mistake this concept of love for a feeling or an emotion, the type of love meant by the Greek word *eros*, which refers to a desire for one's own pleasure. The unconditional love we are speaking of here is denoted by another Greek word, *agape*, a love that gives but expects nothing for itself. In the New Testament, *agape* is used to describe God's love of us,

---

2. Søren Kierkegaard, *Works of Love*, trans. Howard and Edna Hong (New York: Harper Torchbooks, 1962), p. 55.

our love of God, and our love of neighbor. This is the love on which Christian morality is founded.

Now some will understandably argue that an ethic of selfless love subjects Christians to an unreasonable or disadvantageous burden in the competitive arena of business and professional life. Isn't there some truth in Carr's warning that "religious idealism" is a weakness in a business world that does not reward kindness?[3] Yes, discipleship can indeed be costly, but it is nonetheless possible for an ethic of love to undergird the Christian's life and witness in today's workplace. The practical application of this ethic may be found in God's requirements of justice, kindness, and humility.

"To Do Justice"

Justice begins with upholding the law, but goes much further in protecting the legitimate rights and interests of others. Because all people are created, valued, and loved by God, we must actively work for fairness in a system that is inherently inequitable.

What does justice mean in the business context? In practice, this must be worked out in each circumstance where we are called to act — for example, improving inhumane working conditions and other situations that devalue people; truthfully representing the features and benefits of products and services; ensuring equal opportunity for people of diverse backgrounds; charging fair and reasonable interest to the poor; treating suppliers as you would like to be treated; respecting coworkers as people with lives outside of work; not tolerating sexual harassment in the office; exchanging "a full day's work for a full day's pay."

In the Old Testament, the prophet Jeremiah's concern about unjust treatment of workers leads him to issue a stern warning to King Jehoiakim:

3. Albert Carr, "Is Business Bluffing Ethical?" *Harvard Business Review,* January-February 1968, p. 144.

"Woe to him who builds his palace by unrighteousness,
his upper rooms by injustice,
making his countrymen work for nothing,
not paying them for their labor."

(Jer. 22:13)

The king's indifference to these workers stands in stark contrast to the goodness of God:

"Let not the wise man boast of his wisdom
or the strong man boast of his strength
or the rich man boast of his riches,
but let him who boasts boast about this:
that he understands and knows me,
that I am the LORD, who exercises kindness,
justice and righteousness on earth,
for in these I delight," declares the LORD.

(9:23-24)

Paul Camenisch, a theologian with expertise in business ethics, believes that the church has failed to convey to believers their personal responsibilities for doing justice at work. In a critique of Protestant policy statements on economic justice, he writes, "Seldom if ever are Christians addressed as influential actors responsible in their vocations for seeing that, within their power, justice is done. They are not seriously challenged to ask questions about the human impact of their actions as workers, managers, consumers, and owners on their fellows. . . ."[4] As we have discussed, church pronouncements on economics tend to critique the macroeconomic system with little or no thought to the difficulties faced by individuals or organizations within the system.

4. Paul Camenisch, "Recent Mainline Protestant Statements on Economic Justice," *Annual Meeting of the Society of Christian Ethics* (1987): 72.

"To Love Kindness"

We are to be kind to others, of course; but even more important, we are to *love* kindness, just as the Lord delights in it. This speaks to our attitudes and motivations, for God examines our hearts as well as our actions. Christian kindness must be a sincere commitment to the well-being of others as a reflection of God's love for us.

Justice and mercy are sometimes seen as mutually exclusive, but this is not so in Christian ethics. Biblical teachings recognize the necessity of judgment and holding individuals accountable, which is part of acting responsibly at work. But this is tempered by an overriding imperative to love others, even those who seem undeserving of love. Unlike business metaphors describing competition as "all-out war" or "survival of the fittest," Jesus' teachings suggest that we should even love our competitors and others who wish to defeat us:

> "If you love those who love you, what credit is that to you? Even 'sinners' love those who love them. And if you do good to those who are good to you, what credit is that to you? Even 'sinners' do that. And if you lend to those from whom you expect repayment, what credit is that to you? Even 'sinners' lend to 'sinners,' expecting to be repaid in full. But love your enemies, do good to them, and lend to them without expecting to get anything back. Then your reward will be great, and you will be sons of the Most High, because he is kind to the ungrateful and wicked. Be merciful, just as your Father is merciful." (Luke 6:32-36)

If to be kind — *to love kindness* — is to emulate God, we must not mistake kindness for weakness. Christian disciples are to challenge policies or actions that may allow harm to come to others. Intervening on behalf of another, perhaps by raising an uncomfortable question, can be a difficult act of kindness. The Bible describes kindness in many forms, including helpfulness, forgiveness, generosity, patience, compassion, and sympathy. Who would deny that these are sorely needed in today's workplaces?

As Christians we are to be available to God as instruments of kindness, mindful that despite our limited capacities for this, "it is God who works in you to will and to act according to his good purpose" (Phil. 2:13). Accepting that we cannot do it alone inspires humility and ensures that the good we do for others is neither condescending nor self-congratulatory. Paul counts kindness among the fruits of the Spirit that attest to Christian authenticity (Gal. 5:22).

"To Walk Humbly"

Old Testament theologian Walter Brueggemann notes that the Hebrew word for "humble" used in the Micah passage occurs only one other time in the Old Testament, in Proverbs 11:2: "When pride comes, then comes disgrace, but with humility comes wisdom." Pride and humility are two contrasting attitudes with predictable consequences. "Thus the phrasing of Micah answers the question 'How to walk' by calling attention to the need and inescapability of the others who walk with us on the path of life."[5] The humble enjoy God's companionship, but the prideful walk alone.

In psychology and other fields, pride is synonymous with self-esteem and self-sufficiency, which are deemed worthy goals. But in theology, pride refers to the idolatrous self-love that often motivates attempts at self-sufficiency and denies God's rightful place in our lives — the place of the highest good. Augustine calls the prideful "self-pleasers" and sees "something in humility which, strangely enough, exalts the heart, and something in pride which debases it."[6] Pride blinds us to moral failures for which we need to repent, frequently prompting attempts to justify our actions solely against the narrow requirements of the law.

---

5. Walter Brueggemann, "Walk Humbly with Your God," *Journal for Preachers* 33, no. 4 (2010): 15-16.

6. St. Augustine, *The City of God*, in *The Works of Aurelius Augustine, Bishop of Hippo*, vol. 2, trans. Marcus Dods (Edinburgh: T&T Clark, 1871), pp. 25-26.

Indeed, Paul's teaching on pride is interwoven with warnings against using legalistic justifications to convince ourselves of our own righteousness (Rom. 3:27-28; 1 Cor. 1:29; 3:18-21; Phil. 3:3-6).

It is ironic, I think, that Christians who try hardest to live their faith at work are often vulnerable to spiritual pride and self-righteousness. This is a danger zone for those who strive to prove that they are more Christ-like than others. We may be reminded of the parable of the Pharisee and the publican (Luke 18:9-14), where the Pharisee prays, "God, I thank you that I am not like other men — robbers, evildoers, adulterers — or even like this tax collector." Jesus makes it clear that the Pharisee, a sincere and earnest believer, is blind to his own sin. I wonder how many of us have read this parable and prayed, "Thank you that I am not like that prideful, hypocritical Pharisee."

As we saw in Chapter Three, pride goes hand in hand with the pursuit of riches. It is easy to fall prey to an illusion of becoming self-sufficient through the accumulation of material wealth. Moreover, those who attain financial means can easily convince themselves that they are the authors of their own success, "self-made" and beholden to no one else. They forget that they are products of the families and teachers who prepared them, the employers who gave them career opportunities, as well as colleagues, mentors, and other factors made possible by God. Equally dangerous is the belief that financial success proves one has found special favor with God, perhaps because of superior faith or good works. The implication of this prideful illusion is that the woman who labors in the chicken-processing plant is somehow less favored by God.

We are told that Abraham was a wealthy man who enjoyed much business success, but understood that everything he had was an undeserved gift from God. He knew he was blessed for a reason: so that he could bless others. God said, "I will bless you; I will make your name great, and you will be a blessing" (Gen. 12:2).

Envy and jealousy also are unhealthy manifestations of pride in the workplace, as when we artificially elevate our own interests and self-esteem by denigrating the worth of others. Within every organization there are those who feel it is their loss when someone else succeeds. "She doesn't deserve that promotion." "He's the boss's favorite." The envious person, Aquinas says, "grieves over the good of those who are deserving of it."[7] Envy and pride are among the Seven Deadly Sins, just as humility is one of the "contrary virtues" that stand opposite them.

The call for humility is pervasive in the Old Testament, resounding especially in the tragedies of kings and other leaders whose pride leads to personal destruction. But it becomes a central theme and an explicit requirement in the New Testament. Paul counsels the Philippians, "Do nothing out of selfish ambition or vain conceit, but in humility consider others better than yourselves," reminding them of the character of Jesus, who "humbled himself and became obedient to death — even death on a cross!" (Phil. 2:3, 8). James echoes the proverb when he speaks of the "humility that comes from wisdom" (James 3:13), and Peter exhorts Christians to "clothe yourselves with humility toward one another . . ." (1 Pet. 5:5). Jesus himself contrasts self-aggrandizement with humility: "For whoever exalts himself will be humbled, and whoever humbles himself will be exalted" (Matt. 23:12). We see the truth of this when people are admired for selfless gestures, such as giving a coworker credit that they might have taken for themselves. We also see that false humility is easily recognized as prideful hypocrisy.

Walking humbly is the third point in Micah's text, but in practice it is a precondition for the first two. Doing justice, which often means acting with impartiality, requires the humility to see others in the same light as ourselves. True kindness frequently means setting aside our own interests for others' sake. Though humility is akin to modesty, it should not be confused with a lack of self-respect or poor self-esteem. On the contrary, standing against injustice or acting selflessly for others takes confidence that comes from trusting God.

Valuing others at least as much as we value ourselves is an attitude born of honest self-critique. Through the wisdom that comes

---

7. St. Thomas Aquinas, *Summa Theologica*, vol. 1 (Charleston, S.C.: BiblioLife Network, 2008), p. 474.

from humility we learn to see our own shortcomings and to welcome constructive input from others. "The way of a fool seems right to him, but a wise man listens to advice" (Prov. 12:15). "He who listens to a life-giving rebuke will be at home among the wise" (Prov. 15:31). Self-understanding does not lie *within* us; rather, we can only begin to understand ourselves through the eyes of others *beyond* ourselves. Most important, as Calvin might say, self-knowledge increases with our knowledge of God, not only through personal experience, but through learning about the God known to ancient Israel and to believers through the ages.

For the Christian, honest self-evaluation prompts repentance, which leads to forgiveness, changed behaviors, and a restoration of *wholeness,* the literal meaning of the word *integrity.* Indeed, repentance is incomplete without these actions. Not insignificantly, *humble* comes from the same root word as *grounded,* which is a helpful way to think of having one's feet planted firmly on the ground.

It was my privilege to facilitate a retreat of South African university leaders who gathered to re-envision the role of higher education in promoting ethical leadership for that troubled region of the world. Joining us was Archbishop Emeritus Desmond Tutu, who spoke passionately of the need for public leaders to "hold power lightly" and to recognize when their own conduct is a hindrance to those they lead. On our last day, we adopted a declaration calling for universities to more intentionally cultivate the moral character of students. Here are a few of the attributes the delegates deemed necessary for leaders in today's society:

- *Humility, altruism, and selflessness*
- *Willingness to suffer for the sake of others*
- *Willingness to step aside when ethical considerations require it*
- *Critical self-understanding of personal strengths and weaknesses*
- *Willingness to accept critique and to engage in debate*[8]

8. "A Call for Change and Action," Stellenbosch Seboka on Higher Education and Ethical Leadership, available online at http://wwwo.sun.ac.za/ssel/.

An Ethic of Love and Responsibility

So we see that justice, kindness, and humility are essential elements of love. These three sum up God's moral requirements and serve as practical guideposts on the way to becoming the people we ought to be: responsive instruments for helping the world become as *it* ought to be. We take Jesus as our model for this transformative work, trusting in God to empower us to love with integrity. For Gedeon Josua Rossouw, this is the foundation of a realistic ethic for living the Christian life at work:

> A Christian ethic that stands on this basis is personal, but not private. It is an ethic which, when challenged, does not have to retreat to the safety of the private sphere, because a Christian ethic is based on the conviction that its interpretation of reality is the best available understanding of reality — the one that will make the fullest development of human potential possible.[9]

This potential includes the capacity for genuine responsiveness in all relationships, for authentic discipleship is a process of learning to enact Christian love in every circumstance. H. Richard Niebuhr (Reinhold Niebuhr's theologian brother) proposes that responsibility is defined chiefly by how we respond to others, including God. This concept of responsibility as *response-ability* may be a better way to think about ethics than adherence to abstract moral principles, compliance with rules, or even achievement of good outcomes. The responsible Christian must be fully attentive to the "decisive present" and the possibilities of God's activity through the lives of others.[10] In responding to them in love, Peter Baelz reminds us, we are in fact responding to God:

> Without this affirmation the command to love becomes a piece of nonsense. With this affirmation it may become a divine-

---

9. Gedeon Josua Rossouw, "Business Ethics: Where Have All the Christians Gone?" *Journal of Business Ethics* 13 (1994): 564.
10. Rossouw, "Business Ethics," p. 566.

human possibility, an invitation and challenge, a promise of forgiveness and renewal.[11]

Niebuhr suggests that responsibilities are discerned continuously as we ask, "What is the fitting response to what is happening?"[12] "Fitting responses" can only be based on justice, kindness, and humility in a spirit of unconditional love. God grants us freedom to respond, to act as moral agents even within businesses or other organizations that constrain us. But we are not freed so that we may act solely on the basis of our own judgment. Our Christian vocation is to be lived out through an ethic of love and responsibility resting on the three pillars of Micah 6:8.

The responsibility to love stands both within and above the larger constellation of duties that come with our particular jobs. It also tends to expand those duties, making it harder to rationalize that certain things are "not my responsibility." Furthermore, an ethic of love and responsibility precludes *irresponsibility* at work.

To be sure, it is easier to live by this ethic in a workplace where these values are encouraged and rewarded. Christian leaders of organizations have a special responsibility to ensure that their priorities encourage individual behavior that is just, kind, and humble. Fortunately, a sound business rationale for this is found in research showing that these values are among the key attributes of employers that attract and retain conscientious employees and excel in customer satisfaction.[13]

On the other hand, there are organizations that actually reward conduct we might deem irresponsible. Many people in otherwise "good" workplaces experience pressure to compromise values in order to meet deadlines or financial expectations. Christians in these situations may feel they bear a greater — and potentially more consequential — responsibility for modeling exemplary conduct.

11. Peter Baelz, *Ethics and Belief* (New York: Seabury Press, 1977), p. 111.

12. H. Richard Niebuhr, *The Responsible Self: An Essay in Christian Moral Philosophy* (New York: Harper & Row, 1963), p. 67.

13. See Robert Levering, *A Great Place to Work: What Makes Some Employers So Good (and Most So Bad)* (New York: Random House, 1988).

Making Responsible Decisions

An ethic of love and responsibility requires that we take into account the legitimate interests of all who may be affected by our actions — even when these interests conflict with one another, as they often do. Few of the dilemmas reported by our research subjects could be reduced to neat choices of right over wrong, good over bad. Nor were they problems where rules could determine the best course of action. The inherent difficulty in most of the cases involved conflicting values and priorities.

Alan the architect knew it was right to protect his employees' jobs; yet he also felt a responsibility to his client, who was struggling to pay his own bills. This was not a clear choice between right and wrong. It pitted right against right, good against good. For Alan the challenge was to discern the *most right* thing to do, while striving to act justly and kindly toward all. He grasped this intuitively, which is why he was disappointed by his pastor's attempt to oversimplify the challenge.

In today's multifaceted business and professional organizations, it is more important than ever to consider multiple interests when making decisions. Although it is not always possible to strike a balance with appropriate weight given to the needs of all involved, decision-makers can learn to be more intentional about discerning the full scope of their responsibilities. This requires taking time for reflection and discussion with others — not an easy thing to do in today's time-pressed workplaces.

The general counsel of a major investment bank told me that his firm's managers get more than two hundred e-mail messages each day. "Some of those call for decisions," he said. "And some of those decisions can have real consequences for our business." He fears that in their haste to deal with a relentless stream of messages, these managers will fail to consider the wider and long-term implications of their decisions. "How can we train them to recognize which decisions require a little more time and maybe a face-to-face conversation?"

This is the nature of work for many people today. The quality of decisions suffers under a cognitive load of constant distractions, multitasking, and time pressures that stretch mental bandwidth to the limit. This is a primary reason why conversations about ethics so often arise *after* the fact, when something has gone wrong as a result of short-sighted decisions.

To counter this, we must cultivate the mental and spiritual discipline to be fully present and aware at work. We must ask deeper questions and take time to seek input from others in important decisions. (See the list of questions on pages 114-15.)

Being a Christian does not automatically qualify one to make superior ethical decisions. In fact, many believers make very poor decisions, while many nonbelievers have the ethical sensitivity and judgment to make very good decisions. We should not be surprised by a large measure of ethical consensus with non-Christians, which may be a reminder that God's requirement to "do justice, love kindness, and walk humbly" is intended for all people.

This being the case, one might reasonably ask why we need *Christian* ethics when other sources of moral guidance may also yield good results. The short answer is that a Christian ethic of love and responsibility is not only about what we *do;* it is about who we are called to *be* in relationship to God. It defines our primary vocation as disciples seeking to be more like Christ — people of integrity (wholeness) at work and in every other area of life. A Christian ethic also points us to ultimate reasons for acting morally, providing a firmer ground and greater motivation than can be derived from reason and experience alone.

In *The Power of Ethical Management,* a book by Ken Blanchard and Norman Vincent Peale, there is the story of a pastor who advises a stressed-out businessman, "When you have patience, you realize that if you do what is right — even if it costs you in the short run — it will pay off in the long run."[14] This advice is thought to be axiomatic by people who vow that "good ethics is good business" or that one will always "do well by doing good." This is often, but not always, true. However, self-interested utilitarianism is not the motivation for a Christian ethic of love and responsibility, which

14. Kenneth Blanchard and Norman Vincent Peale, *The Power of Ethical Management* (New York: William Morrow & Co., 1988), p. 60.

may require taking some actions with no expectation of a financial payoff in the short run or the long run. The Christian imperative to love is a response to God's love for us. Therefore, Christian ethics may or may not yield outcomes that harmonize with the bottom-line aims of business.

James Gustafson, a student of H. Richard Niebuhr and an influential thinker in contemporary Christian ethics, stresses that a Christian ethical perspective gives shape to certain values and moral ends, and it is this, rather than utilitarian motives, which should impel Christians to act with love and responsibility:

> This "loving" perspective is likely to color the things Christians value and approve of in their perception, interpretation, and choices in the world. That which restores and brings life and joy is to be preferred to that which destroys and brings death and suffering and pain, for example. Not only in his rational discriminations, but in his moral sensitivities, the Christian is likely to be sensitive to oppression and injustice, to physical and mental suffering. Christians are likely to interpret not only what is the case, but what ought to be the case in light of the valuations that are determined by the perspective or posture of their faith.[15]

The Necessary Role of the Church

We sometimes mistakenly speak of moral discernment and action solely as individual responsibilities. It is easy to empathize with the overburdened manager alone at her desk praying for guidance about a thorny problem. Yet this need not — and should not — always be so, for the biblical ideal is a *community* of faith, and it is this community that actually makes it possible for individuals to take their faith into the public arena. To this end, at least five facets of the church community are indispensable to individual believers in the sphere of work.

15. James Gustafson, *Theology and Christian Ethics* (Cleveland: United Church Press, 1974), p. 114.

**Making Morally Responsible Decisions at Work:
Some Questions to Consider**

Justice, kindness, and humility are foundational to an ethic of love and responsibility. But how can we apply these values in practical ways? Here are several questions that may be helpful when facing difficult decisions.

- **What's really going on?** Problem analysis must be adequate to the complexity of the situation, as the quality of decisions reflects our interpretation of events, including the actions and intentions of others. This requires time for careful thought and investigation.

- **What makes this decision difficult?** The key to every ethical problem lies in identifying what makes it a problem in the first place. It may be that the interests of different people are in conflict, or that a choice pits important values against each other (e.g., kindness and truth-telling, justice and mercy, short-term gain and long-term good).

- **Who has a legitimate stake in how this matter is resolved?** Business decisions tend to respond most readily to those directly involved, but for this reason the interests of others, especially those with less power or influence, get overlooked.

A Community of Moral Discernment

Jesus told his followers, "I have much more to say to you, more than you can now bear. But when he, the Spirit of truth, comes, he will guide you into all truth" (John 16:12-13). This was fulfilled at Pentecost, although we cannot always discern the Spirit's guidance on our own, for pride and self-interest distort every person's judgment to some degree. The church, therefore, must be a people who pray together, learn from one another, and collectively seek confirmation of God's will. This cannot be achieved through the preached word alone; it requires serious interaction with others through whom God may

- **Am I acting in humility, or are my own interests crowding out the interests of others?** It is natural for decisions at work to favor the interests of the organization and the individual decision-maker. An attitude of humility permits us to step outside ourselves for a more objective view.

- **To whom and to what am I responsible?** Our jobs often entail multiple duties and obligations. A marketing decision, for instance, may involve weighing responsibilities to one's employer, customers, suppliers, coworkers, even competitors. How may these duties be honored while adhering to the transcendent moral requirements of Christian vocation — our responsibility to God?

- **What options are available, and what outcomes may result from each?** Good decision-making identifies and weighs all reasonable alternatives and considers the longer term or broader consequences of each. How might this decision promote justice and kindness for all concerned?

- **Have I sought God's will?** Prayer, Scripture, and the discernment of other believers are means of seeking God's guidance when making tough decisions. Even when God's will remains unclear, we may be guided by a Christian ethic of love and responsibility.

work for our good. We must hone our capacities for objective moral discernment within a community of believers who share a desire to be guided by the Spirit to live faithfully at work. This role of the church is as much about building individual character (who we are in Christ) as about guiding actions (what we do as Christ's representatives), for in developing spiritual and moral maturity, we become more sensitive to God's leading (Heb. 5:11-14).

The church community is also vital to discernment because it is often hard to distinguish what God is doing from everything else that is happening in a given situation. "Furthermore," says Peter Baelz, "even if we are right in thinking that it is possible to discern the main thrust of the divine activity, we are still faced with the particular problem how we are to respond as individuals in this or that particular situation."[16] Moral discernment thus moves from understanding the situation, to seeking God's will, to choosing the best response — all of which are better done with the help of others than alone.

A Community of Moral Discourse

Not surprisingly, discerning God's will as a community does not always yield consensus, especially with the complexity of many moral questions. Perhaps everyone agrees that Christians should act justly and kindly, but what exactly is a just and kind response in a given situation? Is it unjust to pay a single mother the minimum wage, which may not suffice to support herself and her children? Some may argue that anything less than a living wage (based on the realistic local cost of living) exploits people who have few alternatives. Others may counter that it is enough of a good for the employer to provide jobs that would not exist otherwise. In another context, is it unkind for a salesperson to withhold information from a customer about a product's shortcomings? Responses to this question may hinge on the nature of the product, the seriousness of the problems, and the risks facing the buyer.

"At the level of particular problems, Christians do not always speak with a united voice," Baelz notes,[17] which is all the *more* reason why we should foster moral discourse within the faith community. By debating the thornier issues of business and professional life, we broaden our perspectives and re-examine our self-understandings and defining stories. If the church is not the place for honest moral questioning and discourse, what is?

16. Baelz, *Ethics and Belief.*
17. Baelz, *Ethics and Belief.*

A Community of Moral Influence

Businesses and other organizations may use their power for the benefit of some and the detriment of others. There are times when Christians must actively advocate change or seek justice for those who are harmed or excluded by the system. Yet individuals who wish to rectify things often find they lack the know-how and influence to overcome institutional indifference and selfishness. The power of the status quo can overwhelm even those with the best intentions.

For this reason it is a shared responsibility of the faith community to envision and promote just institutions in all employment sectors. History shows that the collective efforts of the church can be far more effective than those of individuals. For instance, the United Methodist Church was among several mainline Protestant denominations to adopt a social creed in 1908 calling for workplace reforms, including the abolition of child labor, protection of workers from dangerous machinery and conditions, a reasonable number of hours in the workweek, and a living wage, among others. The influence of Protestant and Roman Catholic congregations in the twentieth century was instrumental in many such changes, including outlawing racially discriminatory employment practices. Today the church's influence is making a difference on behalf of laborers and communities in the developing world, often by awakening the public conscience and pressuring policymakers in business and government. As it does so, however, it must not neglect its immediate duty to intervene on behalf of those suffering from injustice in the United States and other developed countries.

The Swiss theologian Emil Brunner sums up this responsibility succinctly:

> It is the duty of the church to . . . help bring about a better economic community. And, if she is well advised, she knows that in this work she can join forces with all those of good-will, whether Christian or non-Christian. . . . It is the duty of the church — not of the church alone, but still of the church above

all — to revive the idea of the responsibility of all for all, the idea of concrete responsibility in mutual unity; for only out of this thinking and willing can a new order be created, which — while it certainly is not the Kingdom of God — does deserve to be called a "better" economic order.[18]

A Community of Moral Encouragement

Biblically and historically, the church has been a mutually encouraging community, beginning with the early Christians, who relied on one another to resist and cope with the oppression of the Roman Empire. The writer to the Hebrews exhorts them, "Let us not give up meeting together, as some are in the habit of doing, but let us encourage one another . . ." (Heb. 10:25). Paul advises the church at Thessalonica, "Therefore encourage one another and build each other up, just as in fact you are doing" (1 Thess. 5:11). How many congregations heed this admonition by encouraging the beleaguered managers and professionals in their midst? The greatest need for a supportive church community may be in less stable communities where unemployment is high and wages are low.

For any of us, the encouragement of the faith community is crucial in times when God seems distant. Like the poets and prophets of old, who lamented God's silence in times of trial, all believers experience periods when prayers seem to go unanswered. It is at such times that the church must reassure us of God's love, continuing presence, and past faithfulness. This is also when God may choose to speak to us through the community of believers.

18. Emil Brunner, *The Divine Imperative* (Philadelphia: Westminster Press, 1947), p. 430.

A Community of Moral Example

Finally, the Christian ethic of love and responsibility must begin in the church. On the very evening when he was betrayed by one of his disciples, Jesus said, "A new command I give you: Love one another. As I have loved you, so you must love one another. All men will know that you are my disciples, if you love one another" (John 13:34-35). Sadly, few institutions rival the church for the bitterness of its fights and divisions.

The church must demonstrate to the world that there is an alternative to injustice, indifference, and selfishness. It must strive to model this in all areas of its life and work, including its employment and financial practices. Does the church treat its employees as it would have others treat their employees? Does it manage its financial resources well? If it fails to practice what it preaches, it can expect to have little influence. Remember the people we interviewed who said they would never seek work-related advice from a pastor because the church handles its own business affairs so poorly. (A more extreme aspect of this perception was confirmed by researchers at Villanova University, who found that 85 percent of Roman Catholic dioceses experienced cases of embezzlement in a five-year period.[19]) We must demand the highest standards of integrity and competence in organizations that purport to represent the Christian faith to the world.

The church's ultimate purpose is to proclaim the gospel. This is not merely an institutional or programmatic mission. Every Christian is called to make tangible God's love and redemption through the living of his or her public life. In Brunner's words, "Genuine faith, and love which arises from such faith, is the only creative and regenerating force in the sphere of economic ethics."[20]

19. Robert West and Charles Zech, "Internal Financial Controls in the U.S. Catholic Church," *Journal of Forensic Accounting* 9 (2008): 129-56.
20. Brunner, *The Divine Imperative*, p. 438.

Questions to Consider

- Is it possible to be an aggressive competitor in business while at the same time treating others with kindness and love?
- Good decisions often require time for prayerful reflection and conversation with others. How can we accomplish this in today's time-pressed world?
- This chapter concludes with five essential dimensions of the church community. Where do you see opportunities for the church to improve its performance in these areas?

CHAPTER SEVEN

A Workplace Awakening

It was September 12, 2001, and a senior executive of a major tele-communications company reached me on my mobile phone. Could I recommend a pastor to lead an ecumenical prayer in a quickly organized teleconference for employees? With the nation reeling from the terrorist assaults on the World Trade Center and the Pentagon, the firm's CEO wanted to speak to his more than 75,000 employees and felt it important to include a prayer.

I wondered momentarily if I had heard the question correctly, knowing full well that a teleconferenced prayer at this publicly held company would have been unthinkable on September 10. In the hours after the 9/11 tragedy, barriers to faith in many American workplaces fell as quickly and unexpectedly as the towers in lower Manhattan. Employees gathered to pray in conference rooms and teachers' lounges, on loading docks and construction sites — often spontaneously, but sometimes at the urging of employers. There was, so it seemed, a new openness to faith at work.

Hindsight shows that this would not continue, as most workplaces returned to business as usual. Some employers even found new reasons to fear religion at work, as legal and media attention turned to the plight of Muslims harassed by coworkers, a problem described by one of our interviewees, whose hospital employed several Arab-American physicians.

Yet something *was* changing, and it had begun well before 9/11.

Just three weeks earlier, *The Washington Post* reported on a new openness to religious expression in many companies.[1] In July, the cover of *Fortune* magazine featured the words "God and Business" emblazoned in white letters across a blue sky, announcing a thirteen-page story that described how "a groundswell of believers is breaching the last taboo in corporate America." Managing editor Rik Kirkland wrote in his introduction to the issue that he had never expected to see those words on the cover. "At *Fortune* our articles of faith are limited to belief in free trade, unfettered competition, and the proposition that capitalism works best when companies stick to creating value for shareholders. Our normal beat: mammon."[2] The issue was a best seller.

As early as 1999, a *BusinessWeek* cover declared "religion in the workplace" the latest trend. "Gone is the old taboo against talking about God at work," declared the report in something of an overstatement. "In its place is a new spirituality, evident in the prayer groups at Deloitte & Touche and the Talmud studies at New York law firms. . . ." It documented activities from traditional Bible studies to New Age practices to show that religious expression was increasingly common and condoned at work.[3]

A Movement of the Laity

Throughout the 1990s, Christians in many parts of the world were joining the movement to integrate faith and work. As the new century dawned, the shock of 9/11 and widespread disillusionment about corporate America fueled even more interest. Today the movement is flourishing, aided greatly by social media and globally networked organizations, yet without much in-

---

1. Bill Broadway, "Good for the Soul — and the Bottom Line," *The Washington Post*, 19 September 2001, A1.

2. Quoted by Marc Gunther, "God and Business: The Surprising Quest for Spiritual Renewal in the American Workplace," *Fortune*, 9 July 2001, pp. 58-80.

3. Michelle Conlin, "Religion in the Workplace," *BusinessWeek*, 1 November 1999, pp. 150-58.

volvement by the institutional church. Indeed, many of today's most successful work-related ministries were born out of frustration with the church and its failure to respond to an obvious need and opportunity.

The rise of this trend is well-documented by Princeton University's David W. Miller in his book *God at Work*. He concludes, "The church and the theological academy have a choice: they can sit on the sidelines, ignore the movement, and let it pass them by, or they can learn from it, engage it, and help shape the theology and practice of faith at work."[4] As the movement gathers momentum, especially among evangelical Christians, it is impossible to know the full scope of a phenomenon comprising everything from informal prayer groups in the corners of employee cafeterias to company-paid chaplaincies to businesses founded as Christian missions.

This surge of interest may be attributed to several advocates of lay ministry in the late twentieth century. William E. Diehl, a Lutheran executive at Bethlehem Steel, inspired many businesspeople with his popular books: *Christianity and Real Life* (1976), *Thank God It's Monday* (1982), *In Search of Faithfulness: Lessons from the Christian Community* (1987), and *The Monday Connection: On Being an Authentic Christian in a Weekday World* (1991). In the last of these, he writes, "The false idols and pernicious values of society remain unchanged unless 'Monday Christians' act and witness to their faith in a relevant manner. Yet most Christians are unable to bring into the experiences of everyday life the basic elements of a faith they profess on a Sunday morning."[5] He set out to rectify this, not only through writing, but by founding an influential organization called the Coalition for Ministry in Daily Life.

Diehl's collaborators included Pete Hammond, who took up the cause through InterVarsity Christian Fellowship, an evangel-

---

4. David W. Miller, *God at Work: The History and Promise of the Faith at Work Movement* (Oxford: Oxford University Press, 2007), p. 153.

5. William E. Diehl, *The Monday Connection: On Being an Authentic Christian in a Weekday World* (New York: HarperCollins, 1991), p. 1.

ical parachurch organization with 860 chapters on college and university campuses in the United States. He established InterVarsity Marketplace Ministries and became one of the most influential thinkers in the movement, showing a knack for connecting people and ideas across the church and workplace spectrum. He saw the "American entrepreneurial spirit" in the grassroots character of many workplace ministries. "We have a long history of rugged individualistic ventures with lots of independent activity full of vision, passion, and adventure. That also means duplication, frequent failures, and competition."[6]

Hammond's program at InterVarsity helped to popularize "marketplace" as a euphemism for the workplace or business sphere. Although many evangelical leaders before and since have embraced this term as if it were a more "Christian" way to speak about work life, it is a regrettable contrivance that further distances faith from work life as most people experience it. Few ordinary businesspeople come home to the greeting, "How was the marketplace today?" The term is even less suitable for the work environments of public employees, educators, non-profit workers, and many other professionals. Hammond ultimately reached this conclusion as well, writing that he "struggled with the limitations of the phrase" before changing the name of Marketplace Ministries to Ministry in Daily Life, reflecting a long-time affiliation with the coalition founded by Diehl.[7] Much of InterVarsity's emphasis today involves a program for MBA students in business schools.

Another seminal shaper of the movement is Howard E. Butt Jr., whose family owns and operates one of the nation's largest private companies, a Texas-based supermarket chain with 315 retail locations. Advocating a blend of evangelism and social justice, he worked with the Billy Graham Evangelistic Association as early as the 1950s to develop the Layman's Leadership Institutes. Butt was

---

6. Pete Hammond, "The Marketplace Movement: A Brief Overview," accessed online at www.intheworkplace.com.
7. Pete Hammond, "What's in a Name?" accessed online at www.intheworkplace.com.

invited by President Dwight D. Eisenhower to speak at a National Prayer Breakfast and later was appointed by President John F. Kennedy to the first Committee on Equal Employment Opportunity. He has authored several books on faith in everyday life, and his sixty-second radio spots, "The High Calling of Our Daily Work," still air on more than two thousand stations. He also established Laity Lodge, an ecumenical retreat center in Texas, and an online ministry for businesspeople, TheHighCalling.org.

Diehl, Hammond, Butt, and others like them erected a platform of ideas that has allowed a multifaceted movement to thrive through the initiative and leadership of laypeople. The institutional church, meanwhile, has been less than enthusiastic about these ideas, preferring to redefine lay ministry as more active involvement in existing church programs. "Whether church professionals never fully absorbed that, by definition, the location of lay ministry was extrinsic to the gathered church or whether they were threatened by a loss of power and control is open to debate," writes Miller.[8]

Lay-Led Ministries

Atlanta investment advisor Kevin Latty was an adult when he became a Christian, but it was not long before he was a leader in a church-based ministry providing critical medical care to children in developing countries. "It was in the third world that I realized *I* was the one who needed ministry," he recalls. Making his living in an industry where many people put their trust in wealth, he saw that businesspeople were reluctant to discuss their problems with one another — even at church. "I don't believe most churches have created environments where people can be authentic." So he decided to fill the void by co-founding Souly Business, an independent ministry that brings businessmen together for weekend retreats where they "don't need to impress others and can be honest about their failures."

8. Miller, *God at Work*, p. 59.

Latty tells of a CEO speaking through tears about a layoff affecting thirty employees. The gatherings are led by business and professional people, not clergy, which, he explains, "actually lends a sense of credibility to it. Our leaders are there because they want to be, not because it's their job." The organization now operates in two southeastern states and has played a role in starting a similar ministry for women. Recalling his earlier volunteer work, he says, "God has given us a place to operate. Why should I go on a mission trip to Africa?"[9]

Farther west, Cincinnati-based At Work on Purpose is led by Chuck Proudfit, a consultant who formerly worked for several major corporations. Like Latty, he was a relatively new Christian in 2003 when he saw a need to form an organization to help Christians "successfully live out faith in a work world that is largely disconnected from God." His motivation was less inspiration than exasperation, he recalls, after realizing that "the local church doesn't deal much with the working reality of most people in their congregations" and often looks at business as a "place to fund ministry, but not a venue for ministry." He likes to ask working Christians, "What unique expression will you bring to the marketplace ministry that is yours — that God is handing you?"[10]

At Work on Purpose takes full advantage of social media and other tools of communication. It has active groups on Facebook and LinkedIn, produces and posts videos on YouTube, publishes a blog, and streams a weekly audio devotional from its Web site. It offers coaching services, convenes roundtable meetings of businesspeople, and sponsors something called "Biznistry" to encourage business-as-mission enterprises. (We will look more closely at this concept below.)

In the Sacramento area, business consultant Aric Resnicke leads an organization that forms "practical and pragmatic co-mentoring groups" of believers with similar business interests. Founded in 2008, Christian Business Roundtable (CBR) invites

---

9. Author's interview with Kevin Latty. See also www.soulybusiness.org.

10. See www.atworkonpurpose.org. Interview with Chuck Proudfit at www.hmsinc.org, "Revelations" video series, episode nine.

business owners, executives, managers, and solo entrepreneurs to meet twice monthly with eight to ten "co-advisors" in cadres led by peers with similar interests. The group stresses that these are not networking events, but sessions where participants "are expected to give their time, share their experience, and be prepared to challenge each other in their businesses and in their relationship with Christ."[11] In addition, CBR maintains an active Facebook page with "friends" well beyond California. In 2009 Resnicke launched Christian Professionals Worldwide, a separate group on LinkedIn, the online social network for professionals. In less than a year it had more than 23,000 members, with subgroups in Australia, Africa, Asia, the United Kingdom, and a number of U.S. cities.

Yet another model of lay-led ministry may be found in the Kansas City area, where Integrity Resource Center (IRC) hosts "Faith Incorporated," an annual conference attended by about five hundred businesspeople who study "biblical business practices, network with other Christian people from the marketplace, and commit to being a follower of Jesus — not just at home but also in the workplace."[12] Founder Rick Boxx, a layman with a background in banking and public accounting, invites Christians to join IRC work by signing a "FIRE" covenant committing themselves to Faith in God ("the owner of all things . . . with authority over any decisions I am personally responsible for . . ."); Integrity (adhering to "rules of honesty, justice, and integrity so that I don't injure or defraud others . . ."); Relationships (treating others with "respect and dignity, including all employees, customers, suppliers, and government officials," modeling "Jesus' two greatest commandments by 'loving God' and 'loving others as ourselves'"); and Excellence (representing "our Lord Jesus in the workplace I will do my work as unto the Lord . . ."). The covenant spells out these commitments and stresses the need to be accountable to other believers in keeping them.[13]

11. See www.christianbusinessroundtable.com.
12. See www.faithincorporated.org.
13. See www.integrityresource.org.

Organizations like these are illustrative of the grassroots approach that has spawned dozens of lay-led ministries in the U.S. and abroad. Some of these are small and geographically defined, others span entire industries or professions, and still more are confined to specific companies. Their priorities vary with the philosophies and interests of their members and may include evangelistic outreach, spiritual support groups, or education in the application of Christian teachings.

Miller points out that this concept is not entirely new, citing the Gideons International as a pioneering initiative of the laity. With 10,000 chapters worldwide, the group is well-known for placing Bibles in hotel rooms, hospitals, and prisons. Less known is its founding in 1899 as the Commercial Travelers' Association of America, a non-denominational society of salesmen with a mission of evangelism and service in the business community.

Thirty-one years later, with the Great Depression taking a toll on Americans' economic lives, another group of laymen formed Christian Business Men's Committee after a local revival in Chicago. By 1937 the organization had a network of groups in cities as far away as San Francisco. Today it continues to thrive as Christian Business Men's Connection, reporting a membership of more than fifty thousand in seventy countries. Although its mission is primarily evangelistic, some activities are aimed at discipleship development, and it has expanded to include a Christian Business Women's Fellowship.

The decades following World War II saw a surge of interest in equipping non-clergy for various ministries. From the World Council of Churches to the Roman Catholic Vatican II Council, calls went out for a more egalitarian ecclesiology permitting more meaningful lay participation in the work of the church. Fresh thinking about lay ministry was a catalyst for a host of new organizations within professional and business fields. An example is the Christian Legal Society (CLS), created to "inspire, encourage, and equip lawyers and law students, both individually and in community, to proclaim, love, and serve Jesus Christ. . . ." Now with thirty-eight chapters across America, CLS is among a number of groups formed by Christians within industries and professions as diverse as law enforcement, medicine, and financial planning; the groups focus mostly on the practical application of Christian beliefs.

There are also general-interest organizations, such as Priority Associates, a ministry of Campus Crusade for Christ International that promises to help business and professional people "see how their faith matters in the day-to-day dealings of the workplace." It has local groups in twenty U.S. cities and in London, England.

An Array of Resources

Much of the impetus for today's movement comes from a burgeoning library of books with titles like *Your Work Matters to God; The Monday Connection; Keeping Faith at Work; The Other Six Days; Jesus, CEO; Believers in Business; The Gift of Work; The Soul of a Business; God Is My CEO; God on the Job; The 9 to 5 Window; God in the Marketplace;* and *Life@Work* (to name but a few). This popular genre comprises thoughtful theological works, autobiographical accounts of business life, devotionals, motivational self-help guides, topical Bible studies, and even fanciful attempts to recast Jesus, Daniel, Nehemiah, and other biblical personalities as modern-day business leaders. As one might imagine, the quality is as varied as the topics.

In 2002 Pete Hammond and two co-editors compiled an exhaustive review of as many books as they could then find on this subject. *The Marketplace Annotated Bibliography: A Christian Guide to Books on Work, Business, and Vocation* identifies more than seven hundred books and other publications in business, government, health, law, the arts, and other fields[14] — a number that has grown significantly in the years since. The bibliography includes a chapter on the development of the faith-at-work

---

14. Pete Hammond et al., *The Marketplace Annotated Bibliography: A Christian Guide to Books on Work, Business, and Vocation* (Downers Grove, Ill.: InterVarsity Press, 2002).

trend, showing how earlier writings on the ministry of the laity have influenced contemporary thought and challenged the status quo as a "highly institutionalized 'churchianity' wrestles with declining numbers, loss of loyalty, declining social authority, and some growing hostility."[15]

The Internet is now the primary engine for the movement's growth, including sales of books and study materials. Global and local organizations use Web sites and social networks to recruit members, deliver services, share ideas, and collaborate with their counterparts everywhere. Several of these groups publish well-read blogs, e-newsletters, and daily devotionals like Integrity Resource Center's *Integrity Moments* and Marketplace Leaders' *TGIF: Today God Is First*. (See Figure 7.1 for examples of online organizations.)

Faith-Based Initiatives in the Workplace

Up to this point, we have considered groups that organize and meet outside of working hours. However, much of the faith-at-work movement actually thrives within places of employment, not only through informal prayer and study gatherings in workplaces of all sizes, but more recently through employer-sanctioned "affinity groups" at major companies like Toyota, Sears, American Express, Intel, Texas Instruments, and Continental Airlines. A case in point is the Coca-Cola Christian Fellowship, co-founded by Steve Hyland, director of the company's North American retail merchandising. More than 270 coworkers attended the first meeting. Hyland says his involvement in the fellowship has taught him to pray, "'God, give me divine appointments during the day. Help me see these people the way that you see them. Help me to be a witness.'"[16]

---

15. Hammond et al., *The Marketplace Annotated Bibliography*, p. 25.

16. Amy Kenna, Amanda Knoke, and Bob Paulson, "God at Work: Is the Church on the Job?" *Decision Magazine*, 1 July 2004 (accessed online at www.billygraham.org).

Figure 7.1. Examples of Lay-Led Ministries Online

- At Work on Purpose: www.atworkonpurpose.org

- Christian Business Men's Connection: www.cbmc.com

- Christian Business Roundtable:
  www.christianbusinessroundtable.com

- Christian Business Women's Fellowship: www.cbwf.org

- Christian Executive Officers (CEO):
  www.christianexecutiveofficers.com

- Christian Legal Society: www.clsnet.org

- Europartners: www.europartners.org

- Fellowship of Companies for Christ International: www.fcci-online.org

- Integrity Resource Center: www.integrityresource.org

- International Coalition of Workplace Ministries:
  www.marketplaceleaders.org/icwm

- MBA Ministry (InterVarsity Christian Fellowship):
  www.mbaministry.org

- Priority Associates (Campus Crusade for Christ):
  www.priorityassociates.org

- Souly Business: www.soulybusiness.org

- The High Calling of Our Daily Work: www.thehighcalling.org

Affinity groups, generally seen by businesses as a means of managing workplace diversity, allow employees to make social connections with peers who share their interests based on race, gender, military service, country of origin, religion, sexual orientation, or other factors. They may organize service projects, help their employers recruit new talent, or even advocate changes in workplace policies. They agree to operate within strict limits in exchange for official status and access to facilities and services during work hours. It is common for companies to impose rules limiting how and where groups may express themselves, and requiring inclusion of any interested employee, regardless of beliefs, as a safeguard against claims of discrimination. Groups with religious purposes are excluded at many companies, including General Motors, which prevailed in a 2005 lawsuit challenging this policy.[17]

Private-sector employers in the United States enjoy more freedom than government agencies in matters of religion. A business may at its owners' discretion adopt an explicitly sectarian mission statement or even promote itself with images like the Christian fish symbol or the Jewish Star of David, provided this does not create a hostile work environment for those who do not share these beliefs. By contrast, public sector employers must strive to maintain a neutral stance under the constitutional "establishment clause" prohibiting state endorsement of a religion. Consequently, they must allow employees appropriate religious freedom while avoiding any official action that may compromise state neutrality. To complicate matters further, the function of a government employee may even affect the extent to which religious expression is permissible. For instance, a schoolteacher's statements are more likely to run afoul of the law than those of a custodian or an accountant.

Even with these strictures, some government agencies have authorized religiously defined affinity groups. Just six days before the tragedy of 9/11, Angie Tracey, a manager at the U.S. Centers for Disease Control and Prevention, secured the agency's quick approval to establish the Christian Fellowship Group. Within hours, a system-wide e-mail announced the news to eight thousand employees, and Tracey's inbox was inundated with e-mails from interested coworkers. "I was dumbstruck," she recalls. The group soon had four hundred members.[18] Her application likely benefited from precedents at

---

17. See Moranski v. General Motors Corp., 433 F.3d 537 (7th Cir. 2005).

18. See Moranski v. General Motors Corp.; see also Os Hillman, "Faith in the 9-to-5 Window," accessed online at www.intheworkplace.com.

other federal agencies. When three employees of the Internal Revenue Service in 1995 sought approval for Christian Fundamentalist Internal Revenue Employees (CFIRE), it took two lawsuits on the employees' behalf to cause the agency to reverse its stance. Today CFIRE has equal status with other affinity groups and has formed chapters in multiple IRS offices.[19] Its fundamentalist statement of beliefs, which all members are required to support, also illustrates how difficult it can be for any one organization to serve all Christians in a workplace.

The Wariness of Employers

Whether or not employers formally sanction religious groups, many remain wary of grassroots efforts to bring faith into the workplace. One skeptic is Frank McCloskey, recently retired vice president of diversity at Georgia Power Company, who questions "the perceived benefits and positive outcomes being credited to more Christian workplace expression" and argues that companies can get better results by "improving and evolving management competencies" without involving religion. The competencies he cites are treating people with respect and inclusion, rewarding collaboration, and reducing fear of retaliation when employees object to management policies or behaviors. "This is not a management challenge that will be resolved with higher levels of Christian faith workplace expression." Furthermore, he contends, "It is unrealistic to think that 'bringing someone's whole self' to work through higher levels of Christian workplace expression will overcome . . . management deficiencies."[20]

It is true enough that expressing one's faith does not necessarily make one a better manager, and it can even have the opposite effect when done in a clumsy or insensitive manner. Nonethe-

19. Allyssa Rosenberg, "Faith First," *Government Executive*, 1 February 2008, accessed online at www.govexec.com; see also www.cfireirs.org.

20. Frank McCloskey, "Religion and Faith at Work: When Does Inclusion Become Exclusionary?" *Insights into Diversity*, September 2010, p. 12.

less, Christians may become better managers and employees if they take seriously their obligations to treat others with justice, kindness, and humility — a form of expression that has less to do with talking about their convictions than striving to live by them. (It was St. Francis of Assisi who memorably advised, "Preach the gospel always; when necessary use words.")

McCloskey warns businesses to beware of Christian employee groups that proselytize or attempt to create opportunities for external ministries to influence the workplace, as this may offend or demean "non-Christian, non-religious, lesbian, gay, bisexual, and transgender employees." In his estimation, Christians constitute the dominant group in most U.S. workplaces, resulting in an atmosphere of "Christian privilege" that already places others at a disadvantage. Corporate leaders, he believes, should be clued-up on the dangers of "'marketplace' Christian organizations whose stated mission and agenda is to Christianize America."[21]

McCloskey's concerns notwithstanding, few employers are well-prepared for the growing complexity of religious issues in the workplace. Most corporate policies are designed to enforce the legal definitions of religious discrimination and harassment. Meanwhile, the greater risks — and opportunities — arise from the need to accommodate employees who insist on spiritual wholeness at work. A move from "park it at the door" to "keep it to yourself" simply will not suffice in today's challenging climate.

Looking forward, many employers can expect to encounter more discomfort with religion. As America and other Western nations become more religiously diverse, employees are demanding new forms of accommodation — dietary restrictions, head coverings, sanitary rituals, regular prayer breaks, prescribed hairstyles (including facial hair), nontraditional holidays, exclusion from certain activities, and so forth — as groups like the Council on American Islamic Relations urge their faithful to assert their rights at work. "Now that other religions are weighing in with their requests, where will it end?" asks Dudley

21. McCloskey, "Religion and Faith at Work," p. 15.

Rochelle, an attorney who represents employers in cases involving religion. An exception or special arrangement to accommodate a Christian observance may create an obligation to do likewise for all religions. "Suddenly, the first accommodation offered becomes a slippery slope for the employer."[22]

The U.S. Equal Employment Opportunity Commission cites federal case law in defining "religion" for employers:

> Religion includes not only traditional, organized religions such as Christianity, Judaism, Islam, Hinduism, and Buddhism, but also religious beliefs that are new, uncommon, not part of a formal church or sect, only subscribed to by a small number of people, or that seem illogical or unreasonable to others. Further, a person's religious beliefs "need not be confined in either source or content to traditional or parochial concepts of religion." A belief is "religious" for Title VII purposes if it is "'religious' in the person's own scheme of things," *i.e.,* it is "a sincere and meaningful belief that occupies in the life of its possessor a place parallel to that filled by . . . God." An employee's belief or practice can be "religious" under Title VII even if the employee is affiliated with a religious group that does not espouse or recognize that individual's belief or practice, or if few — or no — other people adhere to it.[23]

The EEOC Compliance Manual illustrates this with numerous examples, including a supervisor's refusal to accommodate an employee's request for time off to attend the Samhain Sabbat, the October 31 new year observance of Wicca, her religion. The manual advises that the supervisor's refusal "violates Title VII unless it can be shown that her request would impose an undue hardship." The potential for "undue hardship" on an employer is

22. Dudley Rochelle, "Religion in the Workplace: The Challenges of Balancing Productivity and Employee Rights," *Littler Mendelson Partner Advisory,* February 2005, p. 24.

23. U.S. Equal Employment Opportunity Commission, *Compliance Manual, Sec. 12: Religious Discrimination* (Washington, D.C.: Government Printing Office, 2008), pp. 5, 6.

a legally accepted reason to deny an accommodation, though this will not suffice in every case.

Despite these challenges, Rochelle considers it wise to look for creative ways to allow for religious expression and practice at work, reducing the likelihood of lawsuits and fostering better relations with employees. Shipping and logistics giant UPS provided a good example of this when it met the religious needs of Sikh truck drivers by issuing an official turban in the company's familiar brown color. Leadership scholar Douglas A. Hicks proposes that employers aim for a "respectful pluralism" with "a high level of understanding and flexibility on the part of the employer and the co-workers."[24] He explains that this requires seeing people of faith as inseparable from their beliefs; establishing clear boundaries to protect the interests of all; and ensuring that the employer neither endorses nor favors one religion over another.

The Exceptions: Companies Embracing Faith

McCloskey agrees that employers should be faith-neutral and advises them to refrain from hiring corporate chaplains, leaving Christian literature in public places, or citing biblical values as part of a company's mission statement. Yet these are just the sorts of activities that mark a distinctly faith-friendly segment of American business comprising organizations of all sizes in industries as diverse as trucking, health care, and fast food. There is no single approach or philosophy in this niche, for each business embraces faith in its own way.

"Christian-Based Companies"

Go shopping to replace a car battery, and you will likely find products from Interstate Batteries, a private company with an-

---

24. Douglas A. Hicks, *Religion and the Workplace: Pluralism, Spirituality, Leadership* (Cambridge: Cambridge University Press, 2003), p. 176.

nual sales exceeding $1 billion and a distribution network covering every county in the United States. What you may not find on the retail shelf is the company's mission statement, which begins, "To glorify God. . . ." A visit to the company's Web site reveals a business so dedicated to Christian mission that it will help you find not only batteries, but salvation as well. It even suggests the words of a prayer to accept Jesus Christ. There you will read the personal testimony of Norm Miller, chairman of the board, who shares how God helped him overcome past struggles with alcohol. In a more pro-active outreach, the company airs advertisements with the theme "God's Love" on the Dish Network satellite service.

Interstate Batteries is among a number of companies that publicly identify themselves with Christian faith and use their resources to convey the gospel message. Another is Hobby Lobby, an arts-and-crafts retailer with 18,000 employees and more than 450 stores in 39 states. The private firm's annual sales topped $2 billion in 2009, continuing strong revenue growth despite remaining closed on Sundays, one of the busiest shopping days for retailers of its kind. Founder and owner David Green says the policy costs the chain $100 million in lost revenues, but sees it as an important way to honor the Sabbath and respect employees' need for balanced lives. The son of a poor preacher, Green's personal net worth is estimated at $3 billion by *Forbes*, which ranks him No. 316 on its 2010 list of "The World's Billionaires." He and his company are involved in a number of charitable projects, including making substantial gifts in 2007 to retire debt for Oral Roberts University, and in 2009 to purchase land where the C. S. Lewis Foundation plans to build a college.[25]

Like Interstate Batteries, Hobby Lobby devotes some of its advertising budget to promoting the gospel, most notably with full-page ads in local markets on Christmas, Easter, and Independence Day. Its 2010 Easter ad featured the image of a blackboard

25. "The World's Billionaires," *Forbes*, 10 March 2010, accessed online at www.forbes.com; "Hobby Lobby Marks 40 Years of Helping Families Celebrate Life," press release accessed online at www.hobbylobby.com.

with the message "A Slate Wiped Clean." Beneath the words of Acts 3:19 was an invitation to "know Jesus as Lord and Savior" and a toll-free number for spiritual help. The continuous Christian music in every store is another reminder of the company's faith stance, which is articulated as a corporate commitment to "honoring the Lord in all we do by operating the company in a manner consistent with Biblical principles." Among other things, this translates into above-average pay for employees and exclusion of merchandise that it deems contrary to these principles.

Hobby Lobby is often compared to fast-food retailer Chick-fil-A, which never opens its 1,500 restaurants on Sundays yet achieved 9 percent sales growth (to $3.2 billion) in 2009 amid a recession. Founded by chairman Truett Cathy in 1946, Chick-fil-A is a private business that dedicates a portion of profits to the Cathy family's WinShape Foundation, which operates homes for foster children, runs summer camps for disadvantaged youths, and undertakes other projects. The firm's Christian mission is seldom made explicit in its restaurants, nor is Sunday closure promoted as a Christian observance, but employees are reminded of it in many ways, including the company's succinct purpose statement: "Honoring the Lord in all we do by operating the company in a manner consistent with Biblical principles. To have a positive influence on all who come in contact with Chick-fil-A." Known as one of the best places to work in the fast-food industry, it spends close to $2 million per year on college scholarships for its young employees.

These are but a few of the large employers that help define the concept of Christian-based enterprise. Others over the years have included ServiceMaster, Amway Corporation, and Covenant Transport, as well as smaller businesses and professional firms, which researchers say are growing in number.[26] Owners of businesses like these find camaraderie and networking opportunities

---

26. Nabil A. Ibrahim et al., "Characteristics and Practices of 'Christian-Based Companies,'" *Journal of Business Ethics* 10 (1991): 123-32. This article identifies predominant characteristics of these companies and explores their relationships with employees, customers, communities, and suppliers.

in several organizations, including the Fellowship of Companies for Christ International (FCCI), where members "meet in local groups to be equipped, to build relationships, to pray together, and to receive counsel from peers." Since its founding by a group of Atlanta businessmen in 1978, FCCI has grown to include groups in thirty countries.[27] Another organization promising "peer counsel and accountability" is C12 Group, billing itself as "America's leading resource for Christian business owners and CEOs." With chapters in twenty-four states, its home page greets visitors with questions that may resonate with frustrated believers: "Torn between the pressures of daily business and your Christian faith? Sensing a 'shift' in your focus and behavior on Monday vs. Sunday, echoing our culture's artificial secular/sacred divide?"[28]

Corporate and Industrial Chaplaincies

Recognizing that people bring spiritual needs (job-related or not) to work, a growing number of companies employ workplace chaplains to minister to them. Similar to the more familiar chaplaincies of the military, police, and fire services, the practice may have begun in the nineteenth century when ministers in company towns were on factories' payrolls. A 2007 article in *The Economist* describes chaplaincy as a "booming business in America" and estimates that four thousand ministers in business settings are part of "a fad for piety." It asks sardonically, "Are problems at home draining your zest for work? Is your boss a blithering idiot? Then why not consult the company chaplain?"[29]

Chaplaincies may be found at such companies as snack-food maker Herr Foods; poultry processor Pilgrim's Pride; Coca-Cola Bottling Consolidated of Charlotte, North Carolina; auto-service chain American LubeFast; and Tyson Foods, a *Fortune* 500 com-

27. See www.fcci.org.
28. See www.c12group.com.
29. "Praying for Gain: Corporate Chaplains," *The Economist*, 25 August 2007, p. 66.

pany with 117,000 employees in more than 400 plants and offices. Most businesses with chaplains may be categorized as "Christian-based"; but this is not always so. Other employers make the investment for financial rather than spiritual purposes and find that the investment improves employee morale, loyalty, and productivity.[30] Nor are all chaplains Christians, for many large employers recognize that they must offer clergy to people with a diversity of beliefs.

The majority of corporate and industrial chaplains in the United States are supplied on a contract basis by outside firms specializing in these services. The largest by far is Dallas-based Marketplace Chaplains USA, whose 2,400 chaplains in 2010 served 500,000 employees of 418 companies in 43 states. Its smallest client had but one employee.[31] Most professional chaplains have formal training and certification in counseling, with specific skills for employment settings. Continuing education programs are offered by the National Institute of Business and Industrial Chaplains. On call 24 hours a day, chaplains do not engage in overt evangelism, but are on hand to counsel and visit employees who are ill, bereaved, or otherwise in need of spiritual support. For employees with no other minister, chaplains even officiate at weddings and funerals.

A case in point is Allied Systems Holdings, a company with 4,000 tractor-trailer rigs that transport the vast majority of vehicles (more than 9 million per year) from factories, rail yards, and ports to car dealerships in North America. For decades, Allied has placed chaplains at each of its 90 terminals. Retired chairman and CEO Robert Rutland recalls that the program grew out of a "system of core values, which for us meant that we would operate by Christian values. This did not mean that we would evangelize our workforce, but we would manage our workforce

30. See Cathy Driscoll and Elden Wiebe, "Technical Spirituality at Work: Jacques Ellul on Workplace Spirituality," *Journal of Management Inquiry* 16 (2007): 333-48.

31. See www.mchapusa.com. A smaller provider of these services is Corporate Chaplains of America in Raleigh, North Carolina, employing 100 chaplains; see www.chaplain.org.

with love and caring and hope." This was no small task for a company where labor relations with 8,000 Teamsters could be contentious. Today the company attributes its industry-best retention of employees to the chaplaincy.

Rutland believes that the program is especially valuable for truckers who spend so much time far from their homes and families. "We had a driver who had been with us for 25 or 30 years who had a heart attack and died while driving the truck," he says. "We made an impression on his son's mind and spirit by having our chaplains present in that crisis and by reaching out to the family, as well as by having people in management reach out to them." The son grew up to become an industrial chaplain.[32]

Some may find it surprising that business chaplaincies have not prompted much litigation. Allied reports that it has never been sued over its chaplaincy, and its published policy emphasizes, "The Company never forces or coerces any employee in spiritual matters," and "We value diversity, including diversity in religious beliefs."[33]

Business as Mission

Some of today's most ambitious efforts to integrate faith and business are seen in a trend often called "business as mission," or simply BAM, where companies are created for the express purpose of making a profit while simultaneously spreading the gospel, establishing churches, or doing other missionary work. For these social entrepreneurs, capitalism is a better tool than charity for addressing complex problems like health care, education, and hunger. And they find that businesses sometimes are welcome in parts of the world not open to traditional mission groups. According to an article in *Christianity Today* written by

32. Robert J. Rutland, "Have You Hugged a Teamster Lately?" in *Leaders on Ethics: Real-World Perspectives on Today's Business Challenges*, ed. John C. Knapp (Westport, Conn.: Praeger Publishers, 2007), pp. 97-102.

33. See www.alliedholdings.com.

Joe Maxwell, "BAM companies increasingly have a global flavor, creating jobs in developing countries (unlike traditional aid or missions work) and making disciples who carry the gospel to the larger, hard-to-reach community." Maxwell also points out some difficulties that may arise in this kind of work:

> How explicit should ministry efforts be? What sort of spiritual care is a business equipped to offer? Is there a salary range for BAM executives, and can their salaries be too high? Who decides? What happens if a BAM effort goes awry into poor financial or religious practices? When a BAM has to lay people off, how does that affect their view of the gospel? To what extent does a Christian business in an oppressive society actually enable that regime?[34]

One might well ask these questions about any company that claims to have a Christian mission, but BAM enthusiasts insist that their enterprises differ from traditional faith-based companies in the degree to which their resources are "holistically" mobilized for the Great Commission. C. Neal Johnson, dean of a Christian business school and author of *Business as Mission: A Comprehensive Guide to Theory and Practice*, believes that BAM companies distinguish themselves from others by accounting for their performance using four integrated bottom lines: financial, social, environmental, and spiritual. "Measuring those spiritual bottom lines can often be difficult," he confesses, "for kingdom impact is not just measured in terms of good works, as for example, helping disabled people acquire marketable skills and a job." As he sees it, intentionality is the key. "In Kingdom ROI (K-ROI) terms, *why* something is done is equally important as *what* is done. If there is no Christian, God-filled distinctive, then it is no different from a secular good-works program."[35] For

---

34. Joe Maxwell, "The Mission of Business," *Christianity Today,* November 2007, accessed online at www.christianitytoday.com.

35. C. Neal Johnson, *Business as Mission: A Comprehensive Guide to Theory and Practice* (Downers Grove, Ill.: InterVarsity Press, 2009), p. 262.

some skeptics, such a distinction suggests a dangerous secular-sacred divide relegating the work of Christians in other businesses and non-profits to second-class status.

Among the groups promoting the BAM concept are the Business as Mission Resource Team, operating under the auspices of Youth with a Mission (YWAM), and The Lausanne Movement, a global evangelism organization that asks, "How can the church and business work together to develop a theologically sound and holistic view of business'[s] role in the Kingdom of God?"[36] The concept of a built-in funding source for missions has grown in popularity as church mission budgets have been tightened. A case example is Pac Tec Asia Co. Ltd., a data-processing company based in Thailand that uses its profits from commercial sales to build digital libraries of Bibles and other Christian resources for church leaders in the country.[37]

As we unfold the many aspects of the faith-at-work movement, one conclusion is inescapable: More believers than ever are seeking creative ways to integrate their faith lives and work lives, and they are doing it with little help from the institutional church. For many more Christians, the faith-work connection continues to be elusive. In our final chapter we will consider what the church may learn from the faith-at-work movement, and explore some ideas that may help local congregations better engage this vital area of Christian life.

Questions to Consider

- Should Christians encourage their employers to sanction religiously defined organizations at work, even if this means that official status must also be given to groups of atheists, Wiccans, or pagans?

36. See www.businessasmission.com and www.lausanne.org.

37. Rob Moll, "Earning Commissions on 'The Great Commission,'" *The Wall Street Journal*, 12 November 2009, accessed online at www.WSJ.com.

- How is it possible for a company with a Christian mission statement to comply with the letter and the spirit of the laws prohibiting religious discrimination and harassment?
- What might the institutional church learn from faith-at-work organizations led by laypeople? Can you envision specific programs that may be scalable and replicable in a local congregation?

CHAPTER EIGHT

The Church's Potential

In these chapters we have seen how the institutional church often fails working people through its indifference and its incapacity for thinking theologically about their most vexing problems with money, vocation, and moral responsibility. And we have seen that a growing number of believers, undeterred by these shortcomings, are creating alternative modes of ministry beyond the church's traditional sphere. This is encouraging and helpful to many Christians, but how much better would it be if their own congregations actively engaged in ministries to forge strong faith-work connections? How much could we advance the gospel if each of us were encouraged and equipped to live out our common vocation of discipleship in the myriad contexts of our daily work?

As each of my doctoral courses drew to a close, the pastors were tasked with designing new models of ministry to be piloted in their home churches. One, for example, was inspired by the idea that some workers need pastoral care on the job, and so proposed to offer chaplain services to the crews constructing a new shopping mall just down the street from his church. He hoped to gain the cooperation of the mall's developer, a member of his own congregation, by explaining the benefits of chaplains on the work site. He and his classmates had been impressed by our visit with the Reverend Ed Salter, an affable man with an easy smile who served for a number of years as director of chaplain services at Allied Systems Holdings. He told of his experiences at truck terminals where drivers learned to trust him as a confidant with whom they could share their private joys and pains. They found him a reassuring presence far from home. He, in turn, found great satisfaction in the work.

Several others committed themselves to scheduling regular appointments with parishioners to visit their workplaces and learn more about their daily lives, though some harbored doubts about whether they would really be welcome in this unfamiliar territory. We discussed the advice of business ethicist David Krueger, who counsels pastors to approach businesspeople as mutual learners and tells of an educational project where clergy spend a day at work with one or two members of their churches "to see how faith might connect to work in practical ways and also to gain insight into the ethical dilemmas" they face. "In all cases, the executives claim this is the first time their clergy have visited them at work. In most cases, clergy say this is the first time they have set foot in their congregants' workplaces."[1]

Such visits are a good starting point for any pastor, as proven by the personal example of a nineteenth-century minister named Charles Sheldon, whose classic novel titled *In His Steps: What Would Jesus Do?* tells the story of a minister and his congregants as they undertake a one-year experiment to apply Christ's teachings to everything they do, especially at work. Though the best seller's thirty million copies have been an inspiration to people the world over, few readers know the real-life experiences that led Sheldon to preach a series of sermons that was published in 1896 as the novel.

Topeka, Kansas, was in a severe economic recession when Sheldon arrived in 1889 to pastor the Central Congregational Church. To make his ministry relevant to the everyday needs of his parishioners and community, he asked his church for permission to devote twelve weeks to what he called "practical sociological studies," suspending most of his regular duties except

1. David A. Krueger, "Connecting Ministry with the Corporate World," *The Christian Century* 30 (May-June 1990): 572-73.

for preaching on Sunday mornings and Thursday evenings. A remarkable adventure ensued, taking him into every part of town to learn how others lived and worked. He spent a week as a homeless person looking for employment and finding none. He rode with the streetcar crews and stayed with them at their boardinghouse. At the local college, he attended classes with students, helped them study, visited their residence halls, and joined in their ballgames. In a week's time he managed to meet at the local YMCA with nearly every student in the college for "discussion of religious or social subjects," and with most of the faculty as well.[2]

From there, Sheldon turned his energies to the African-American community, where for three weeks he "went into their houses, tried to find out the immediate causes of their destitution," and helped some look for jobs. He visited their schools and had "long talks with the teachers." After getting to know their most prominent leaders, he tested the white community's attitudes by taking a young African-American bookkeeper to dine at several fashionable, white-owned restaurants, and even sending him alone to a particularly high-brow establishment. To Sheldon's surprise, the man was treated with respect at each stop — until at last he was refused membership in the whites-only YMCA.[3]

Sheldon went next to live for a week with the railroad workers — firemen, brakemen, switchmen, yardmen, and engineers — and worked alongside them for no pay while discussing their lives and jobs. Then it was on to the professional community, beginning with the city's lawyers. He interviewed them, read their cases and briefs, and attended their court hearings. At the end of the week he ran a newspaper ad inviting the town's legal establishment to his church to hear a report on his experience and to see if he "treated them fairly." A large number attended.

The following week was similar, but his subjects were doctors

---

2. Charles Sheldon, "Practical Sociological Studies," *The Andover Review* 14 (October 1890): 370-71.

3. Sheldon, "Practical Sociological Studies," pp. 370-71.

whom he accompanied on their rounds. Next came a week with businessmen in real estate, accounting, dry goods, hardware, and other fields. Sheldon questioned them about their treatment of employees and wanted to know if they had profit-sharing plans. Once again, he ended the week with an advertisement, this time inviting the town's businesspeople to a program at the church where he would share what he had learned. "As before, a large number responded and the house was crowded," he reported. The research culminated with a week at the local newspaper, *The Topeka Daily Capital*, where he managed to write several articles and assist with composition, stereotyping, and the printing press.

Sheldon gleaned much from the project, including "an immense amount of valuable material which I cannot but believe will stand me in good stead in the work of my ministry." At a more personal level, he came away "less inclined to judge men harshly or hastily. I find myself from the discipline of those 12 weeks constantly putting myself in the other man's place, and the effect of that is to quicken my sensitiveness to the man's actual needs." For his congregation he foresaw benefits resulting from "the increased knowledge, superficial no doubt, but better than none, of other people's business":

> I know how an airbrake stops a train, and I can describe the process of stereotyping. Now some men might wonder how that could be of any advantage to me in my business as a preacher. But I feel that it is of large advantage. The more I know of a man's business, the better I can preach to him. . . . It makes no difference if I discover by close contact that he is not half so good as I thought he was. I want to know *him*.[4]

Just as the pastors in my doctoral course were moved by their interviews with working people, Sheldon's experience was the impetus to "put into actual motion some of the unapplied power of Christianity; . . . to work as a body and individually to remove the

4. Sheldon, "Practical Sociological Studies," p. 374.

distrust that exists between the workingman and the church."[5] His account of his field research, which appeared in the theological journal *Andover Review,* may be even more inspiring than the novel published six years later.

Now this is not to suggest that most pastors take a three-month sabbatical to experience as many workplaces as possible. But even a few such visits may yield substantial benefits to clergy, not only because they may learn valuable things, but because they will convey a sincere interest in their parishioners' whole lives. And who knows what good may spring from the experience?

Lest we underestimate the impact of Sheldon's project, consider this. Upon learning that black children were woefully behind their white peers in academic achievement, partly because many of their mothers worked during the day to help support their families, Sheldon set out to establish the first African-American kindergarten west of the Mississippi to provide early-childhood care and better education. Among its graduates was Elisha Scott, who went on to law school with Sheldon's help and later gave the name Charles Sheldon Scott to his son, a future lawyer who in 1954 successfully argued the Brown vs. Board of Education case before the United States Supreme Court, effectively ending school segregation in America.[6]

New Perspectives on Ministry

Apart from pastoral visits, what can the institutional church do to support those desiring to apply the "unapplied power of Christianity" in the workplace? Should it replicate the strategies of lay-led ministries that seem to be thriving without its help? The successes of these groups say much about the needs of working Christians, but the church is the center of the faith com-

5. Sheldon, "Practical Sociological Studies," p. 374.
6. Timothy Miller, *Following in His Steps: A Biography of Charles M. Sheldon* (Knoxville: University of Tennessee Press, 1987).

munity and is therefore positioned to achieve things that other groups cannot. A serious emphasis on faith at work may actually be a catalyst for the church's larger mission. In exploring this potential, we should heed the motto of the early ecumenical movement: "Let the church be the church."

What does it mean to be the church in an era when so many are questioning its traditional roles? We may start by thinking afresh about enlivening the moral dimensions of the church proposed in Chapter Five. The faith community should foster *discernment* to understand our situations, to seek God's will, and to take the best actions; promote *discourse* about the thornier issues of work life, sharpening our perspectives and self-understanding; exert *influence* to bring about positive change on behalf of those harmed or neglected by the system; offer *encouragement* of beleaguered workers, managers, and professionals seeking to be faithful in discouraging circumstances; and be an *example* of justice, love, and humility so that the church itself models responsible workplace and financial practices. It is not the purpose of this book to propose a blueprint for changing the church, but any congregation wishing to close the faith-work gap should consider the following four essentials.

Collaborative Leadership

We have seen what lay leaders can accomplish by pouring their energies into ministries outside their own churches. If the culture of the institution is to change, lay leadership will be indispensable in helping the clergy rethink some of the timeworn ecclesiastical assumptions about the priorities of ministry. Even pastors with the best intentions may not be prepared to develop faith-at-work ministries on their own; few possess the know-how, and few congregations are familiar with the concept. Books, continuing education courses, and the examples of existing workplace ministries may be very helpful, but it will take clergy and laity working together to shape a community of disciples leading public lives of meaning. The credibility and insights of lay leadership in faith-at-work ministries cannot be underestimated.

Courageous Conversations

Real change comes grudgingly to any established organization, but this is especially true of churches. It is easy enough to tweak existing programs or add an occasional Sunday school lesson, sermon, or guest speaker, but cultural transformation must begin with honest dialogue about the extent to which the church helps Christians connect faith and work. For many congregations this may amount to what the poet David Whyte calls a "courageous conversation" — one we know we need to have and know we are not having. What do members perceive as the real priorities of the church? What spiritual challenges arise in their own work lives? How do they define vocation and discipleship in weekday contexts? How, if at all, does their faith inform their earning, borrowing, and spending of money? What examples can they give of the church intentionally supporting people in connecting faith and work? Do members trust each other enough to be vulnerable in sharing their personal trials, fears, and failures? Do the clergy and the laity see these things differently?

A similar dose of courage may be needed to discuss how well the church models Christian love and responsibility in its own employment and business practices. Are the staff hired, promoted, and compensated equitably? Is the church exemplary of a good place to work? Is it committed to training and developing employees to their full potential? Do members believe that they have sufficient information about church finances? Is there a stated commitment to appropriate fiscal transparency? Does the church prohibit conflicts of interest, such as business transactions benefiting staff or board members?

These conversations are necessary and will prepare the church for conversations with the larger community. Among my students, a small-town pastor undertook a series of carefully planned dialogues to explore the interplay of Christian ethics and the realities of work, aiming to make the church a safe place for moral discourse, first among members and then with working people in the community. A big-city pastor left the course with a plan to invite the community to regular discussions of faith and business. Held on weekdays in several different business locations, this ongoing project is so successful that it has attracted coverage in the city's daily newspaper.

Redeemer Presbyterian Church in New York City is an inspiring example of what a church can achieve through intentional ministry with working people in its congregation and community. Redeemer's Center for Faith and Work sponsors Vocation Groups to "provide a Christ-centered forum for industry-specific dialogue, fellowship, collaboration, and innovation, to support individual discipleship and cultural renewal." These now include groups in advertising, dance, business, education, entrepreneurship, acting, fashion, filmmaking, the arts, financial services, health care, international diplomacy, writing, and law. In 2008 the church launched the Gotham Fellowship, an intensive nine-month training program to provide young adults working in New York City with the "theological, spiritual, and relational foundations required for meaningful and sustainable integration of faith and work." Each class has twenty-four men and women under the age of thirty, typically from law, finance, government, medicine, education, and the arts.[7]

Relevant Worship

The church's strongest statement about priorities and values is made every Sunday when the faithful convene for worship. Here they are reminded of what must matter most to God. The messages conveyed by most worship services suggest very little about the importance of faith in daily work. What sorts of concerns are lifted up in pastoral prayers? How often do illustrations

7. See www.faithandwork.org.

from work life find their way into sermons? Does the selection of music include hymns or songs with work-related themes? Who is publicly commended for exemplary works of ministry? Do rituals commissioning people for ministry include those whose ministries are their daily work?

For preachers, the greatest test may be letting go of old ideas about calling and vocation. They are the ones who must dismantle the artificial hierarchy that lauds the supposedly higher callings of a chosen few, while implicitly demeaning the honest work of others. Preaching and teaching can be relevant only if clergy stress a shared vocation of discipleship that must be lived out in countless facets of daily life. Just as important, preachers must learn to address the theological difficulty of money as a perennial problem for Christians — a subject that should not be avoided, minimized, or distorted for fund-raising purposes.

Recognizing that relevant resources for worship may not be readily available to many churches, Paul A. Richardson led a group of researchers at Samford University to compile a volume of hymns, prayers, and devotional readings on themes involving vocation and daily living. Included are song titles like these: "How Clear Is Our Vocation, Lord," "Responding to Your Call, O Lord," "All Is Done for the Glory of God," "In Affairs of Economics," and "While Moses Tended Jethro's Sheep." Prayers and reflections are gleaned from sources ancient and contemporary. Funded by the Lilly Endowment through its Programs for the Theological Exploration of Vocation, the volume is prefaced by Richardson, who explains, "In a time in which work and worship — and their relationship — are widely misunderstood as seen from historic Christian perspectives, these materials promote reflection on and expression of a more integrated and coherent approach to life."[8] Any congregation could learn much from undertaking a similar project to identify worship resources relevant to discipleship in work life.

Those wishing to make worship more relevant should

8. *Will You Come and Follow Me?* ed. Paul A. Richardson (Birmingham: Samford University Press, 2007).

thoughtfully evaluate their existing traditions, rituals, formats, music, and other elements, with the goal of eliminating or minimizing anything that perpetuates the false dichotomies of sacred and secular, eternal and temporal, and public and private, which we discussed in Chapter Two. These messages are often subtle and may be implicitly conveyed by what is emphasized or *not* emphasized.

A More Inclusive Narrative

What is the church's story of itself? Who and what are central to the narrative? For a simple test, visit the Web sites of a few churches and notice the images describing the congregations and their priorities. You will likely find many depictions of worship, youth activities, service projects, clergy, and perhaps a foreign missionary or two. Seldom will you see photographs or other descriptions of church members in their weekday work. Too often we reduce the church's rich story to a collection of programs, inevitably dampening the vitality of a community of believers serving Christ through their everyday living.

How different might our understanding of discipleship be if the church's narrative told of bankers, bakers, teachers, and truckers — the living body of Christ in action? Perhaps we would begin to see work life within the scope of a shared Christian vocation, rather than as something "other." One can imagine that if Charles Sheldon were alive today, his church's Web site would find many creative ways to ennoble the daily work of believers. There is arguably no more important issue on the horizon than the church's need to explain itself — to itself and to others — in a way that connects with where real people spend their daily lives.

Faith, Work, and the Future of the Church

As I was writing these concluding words, the pastor of a church in a neighboring city called for advice about starting a program with business and professional people in the community. He explained that the idea was proposed by a young businessman who found his church experience irrelevant to his corporate job. That a younger member felt this way is not surprising, for the millennials are far less willing than their predecessors to divide their lives into two worlds. "Many millennials see their careers and personal life as one," writes Ron Alsop in his book *The Trophy Kids Grow Up.* "They don't talk about balancing work and life but rather about blending them."[9]

This is but one reason the traditional church in America faces a looming crisis as the millennial generation becomes more important to its survival. These young adults are significantly less likely to be affiliated with churches or other religious institutions than were their parents' and grandparents' generations when they were young. About one in four are unaffiliated with any faith at all, including nearly 20 percent of millennials who say that they were raised in a faith tradition.[10] Factoring in the percentage who adhere to faiths other than Christianity, about 40 percent of millennials are unaffiliated with the Christian church.[11] It follows that this generation is also the least likely to attend church services.

These trends are painfully evident in the makeup of the major old-line denominations, where membership has been both declining and aging for four decades. Worried about the future, some churches are undertaking a "large-scale exploration of boundaries," observes Richard J. Mouw, president of Fuller Theological Seminary. "That can be quite frightening, but it is important if we are to be open to new dimensions of ministry. Sometimes I even wonder whether we need to do things in theological education that explicitly invite people to ask parallel

9. Ron Alsop, *The Trophy Kids Grow Up* (San Francisco: Jossey-Bass, 2008), pp. 167-68.

10. *Religion among the Millennials,* research report from the Pew Forum on Religion and Public Life (Washington, D.C.: Pew Research Center, 2010).

11. David Kinnaman and Gabe Lyons, *UnChristian: What a New Generation Really Thinks about Christianity* (Grand Rapids: Baker Books, 2007), p. 18.

questions: 'Hey, would you call this a seminary? Hey, would you call this a theological curriculum?' "[12]

To be sure, the failure to connect faith and work is just one of many reasons the U.S. church is losing its appeal to younger people. Closing this gap will not reverse the continuing marginalization of the church in Western society, but it will make a decisive difference for congregations wishing to remain relevant and for individuals seeking coherence and wholeness. More important, equipping Christians for vigorous discipleship in public life may be the church's best hope for bringing the gospel to a world desperately in need of God's love. And this is reason enough to take seriously the issues we have explored in this volume.

Questions to Consider

- How might your local church begin to explore new avenues of ministry to connect the worlds of faith and work? Who would need to be involved?
- This chapter proposes that congregations need to have "courageous conversations" about ministry priorities and church management practices. Why might it be difficult to discuss these topics openly?
- Does your local church's narrative about itself encompass the full scope of ministry through members' daily lives? Or does it reflect a clergy-centric hierarchy? How might a more inclusive story be conceived and communicated?

12. Joseph E. Hough et al., "Issues and Challenges in Theological Education: Three Reflections," *Theological Education* 37, no. 2 (2001): 107-8.

For Further Reading

The following resources may be useful as you continue to explore the relationship of faith and work.

The Soul of a Business: Managing for Profit and the Common Good by Tom Chappel. New York: Bantam Books, 1994.

The Monday Connection: On Being an Authentic Christian in the Weekday World by William E. Diehl. New York: HarperCollins, 1991.

The Fabric of This World: Inquiries into Calling, Career Choice, and the Design of Human Work by Lee Hardy. Grand Rapids: Wm. B. Eerdmans, 1990.

Keeping Faith at Work by David A. Krueger. Nashville: Abingdon Press, 1994.

Spirituality, Inc.: Religion in the American Workplace by Lake Lambert III. New York: New York University Press, 2009.

Beleaguered Rulers: The Public Obligation of the Professional by William May. Louisville: Westminster John Knox Press, 2001.

God at Work: The History and Promise of the Faith at Work Movement by David W. Miller. Oxford: Oxford University Press, 2007.

Church on Sunday, Work on Monday: The Challenge of Fusing Christian Values with Business Life by Laura Nash and Scotty McClennan. San Francisco: Jossey-Bass, 2001.

A Hidden Wholeness: The Journey toward an Undivided Life by Parker J. Palmer. San Francisco: John Wiley & Sons, 2004.

The Other Six Days: Vocation, Work, and Ministry in Biblical Perspective by R. Paul Stevens. Grand Rapids: Wm. B. Eerdmans, 1999.

God and Mammon in America by Robert Wuthnow. New York: Free Press, 1994.

Called to Holy Worldliness by Richard J. Mouw. Minneapolis: Fortress Press, 1980.

Examples of Respondents' Occupations

Sales manager for a wireless telephone network
Government quality assurance specialist
University transportation and parking manager
Technical support adviser
Telecommunications account manager
Hospital housekeeping manager
Corporate accounting manager
Registered nurse at an elementary school
Insurance agent
Hospital maintenance supervisor
Principal of an advertising agency
Chief executive officer of a family business
Senior manager for a health-care provider
Technician at a nuclear power plant
Investment adviser
Chief executive officer of a retail chain
Bank loan officer
Fund-raising executive for a non-profit agency
College human resources director
Institutional food-services director
Attorney in private practice
Chief executive officer of an assisted living facility
Retired chairman of a publicly held manufacturing company
Car dealer

Vice president of a retail apparel chain
Executive director of a non-profit agency
Principal of an architectural firm
Vice president of human resources for a biomedical research
    company
Grocery store manager
Sales representative for a financial services company
Mail carrier for the postal service
Sales manager for a technology company
Safety director for a bus line
Retail sales clerk
General counsel for a government agency
Quality control specialist for a bank
Registered nurse at a military base
Retired corporate executive
Small business owner
Circuit court judge
Federal law enforcement agent
Financial analyst
Manager at a telecommunications company
Director of a health-care clinic
Laboratory manager
Manager at a computer software company
Newspaper and magazine journalist
Consultant to the energy industry
Computer engineer
Management consultant
Bank manager
Chief financial officer of a public company
Sales representative for a pharmaceutical company
Petrochemical engineer
Human resources manager for a retail company
Restaurant owner
Real estate agent
Federal prosecutor
Physician
Corporate manager

Retired founder/chief executive officer of a consumer products
  company
President of a multinational corporation
Chairman of a Fortune 500 company
President of a bank
Certified public accountant in private practice
United States senator
Human resources director at a public company
Special education teacher
High school teacher
Accounting manager for an architectural firm
Manager of a manufacturing plant
Hospital administrator
Hardware store manager
Executive at an insurance company
Loan technician at a federal government agency
Executive assistant to a bank executive
University program specialist
Child-care worker
Restaurant employee
Truck driver
Administrative assistant for a small business
Senior manager for a cable television company
Executive assistant to a local government official
Pharmaceutical consultant
United States Army officer

Examples of Ethical Issues Recalled by Respondents

Confronting a store manager suspected of theft
Firing an older but under-performing worker
Closing a facility and laying off employees
Confronting workplace peers who use vulgar language
Fearing management reprisals after challenging a policy
Failing to keep promises to customers
Responding to cutthroat competitors
Being urged by a supervisor to hasten an end-of-life decision
    at a nursing home
Deciding whether to hire homosexuals
Feeling pressure from a boss to be dishonest with a customer
Resigning a profitable client who verbally abuses employees
Resolving conflicts among owners of a family business
Being betrayed by a partner who unexpectedly left the firm
    and took key clients
Becoming aware of the employer's attempt to inflate an
    insurance claim
Participating in corporate tax evasion
Making potentially deceptive sales claims
Being asked to backdate transactions to the prior fiscal year to
    improve year-end results
Refusing a bribe as a public official
Witnessing racial discrimination in the workplace
Using bankruptcy as a shield against creditors

Raising executive salaries when rank-and-file workers are
losing benefits
Failing to disclose important product information to customers
Having a friend ask for copies of competitors' proposals in an
RFP process
Using predatory practices with suppliers
Firing a worker for repeated tardiness, then learning she is a
victim of spousal abuse
Deciding whether to resort to a lawsuit for debt collection
Maintaining church/state separation in a public-sector office
Violating the privacy of customers' records
Deciding whether to prosecute a pastor caught shoplifting
Determining a fair price
Being pressured to bypass audit procedures
Objecting to the incongruity between the company's espoused
values and its actions
Struggling with personal guilt about past theft
Selling ads for a cable TV company that offers pornographic
programming
Overworking/burning out employees
Choosing to resign due to lack of support of a decision
Trying to avoid conflicts of interest in rendering investment
advice
Feeling pressure to meet impossible expectations
Seeing potential danger in board members' conflicts of interest
Wondering how to provide work-life balance for working
mothers
Confronting employees about Internet pornography at work
Learning about a falsified employment application after the
hire
Administering a bank lending policy that is unfair to low-
income borrowers
Suspecting a pattern of sex discrimination in hiring
Finding that the employer is indifferent to an unsafe work
environment
Protecting employees' jobs while selling the business to a new
owner

Struggling with whether to confront and/or report a coworker
for alcohol abuse

Making insurance reimbursement decisions that affect
patients' access to treatment

Protecting Arab-American employees from unfair treatment
after 9/11

Objecting to the inequitable distribution of employee bonuses

Hearing the sexual harassment complaint of a coworker

Being asked to cover up an adulterous relationship between
coworkers

Concluding that a product may exploit children

Discovering embezzlement by a senior executive

Responding to a bribery offer by a supplier

Sensing subtle harassment of a person with a disability

Deciding if the company will still support Boy Scouts after
their stance on homosexuality

Falsifying time records for billing purposes

Being asked by a legal client to make false statements

Dismissing a hospital employee for lying to patients

Weighing the consequences of disclosing company financial
problems to employees

Developing wasteful and unnecessary projects to justify
continued grant funding

Opening for business on the Sabbath

Developing advertising for a flawed product

Finding that coworkers are conducting unrelated business on
company time

Concluding that it is impossible to keep a prior promise of no
layoffs

Refusing to pay for substandard work

Discovering a business partner's unscrupulous dealings with
clients

Being wrongly accused of racial discrimination

Finding the employer indifferent to an employee's sexual
harassment complaint

Feeling anger and resentment about losing a job

Trying, as a health-care worker, to be non-judgmental of HIV
   patients
Being asked for a reference on an unsatisfactory former
   employee
Learning of a conflict of interest involving two clients
Making downsizing recommendations in a consulting
   engagement
Feeling pressure to award contracts based on special interests
Manipulating a job description to circumvent discrimination
   laws

Questions Asked by Interviewers

1. Can you describe at least one moral or ethical concern that has affected you personally in your career or work life? (If no answer, go to question 3.)

2. Was the church helpful to you in addressing the concern(s)? If so, how? If not, what might have been helpful?

3. Can you recall specific sermons, classes, or other ways the church has offered practical guidance or help in your business or professional life? Please describe these.

4. Have you ever sought advice or counsel from a pastor regarding a business- or career-related concern? If so, was it helpful? If you have not done so, what considerations might help you determine whether to seek pastoral counsel about a work-related matter?

5. On the whole, do you think the church does enough to help members integrate their faith with their lives at work? If so, how? If not, how might we do better?

Some Occupations of People in the Bible

The Bible is filled with stories of people who made their living in jobs outside the church or temple. Many of the leading personalities in Scripture were farmers, builders, craftsmen, and public officials. The following are examples of these wide-ranging occupations.

Lawyer	Actor	Plasterer
Accountant	Musician	Messenger
Physician	Tailor	Judge
Farmer	Shipbuilder	Governor
Shepherd	Architect	Breeder
Fisherman	Carpenter	Midwife
Tax Collector	Teacher	Cook
Jailer	Blacksmith	Sorcerer
Weaver	Housekeeper	Prostitute
Winemaker	Stonemason	Slave
Sailor	Tentmaker	Poet
Innkeeper	Beekeeper	Artist
Banker	Jeweler	Writer
Soldier	Clerk	Undertaker
Merchant	Scribe	

Index of Names and Subjects

Index of Biblical References